BIGideas

putting the zest into creativity & innovation at work

jonne ceserani

**KOGAN
PAGE**

London and Philadelphia

First published in Great Britain and the United States in 2003 by Kogan Page Limited
Reprinted 2003, 2009

120 Pentonville Road
London N1 9JN
UK
www.koganpage.com

525 South 4th Street, #241
Philadelphia PA 19147
USA

ISBN 978 0 7494 3878 4

British Library Cataloguing-in-Publication Data

A CIP record for this book is available from the British Library.

Library of Congress Cataloging-in-Publication Data

Ceserani, Jonne, 1954-
  Big ideas : putting the zest into creativity and innovation at work / Jonne Ceserani.
    p. cm.
Includes bibliographical references and index.
  ISBN 978-0-7494-3878-4
  1. Creative ability in business. 2. Business communication. I.
Title.
  HD53.C46 2002
  658.4'063--dc21
                                    2002154430

Typeset by Saxon Graphics Ltd, Derby
Printed in Great Britain by the MPG Books Group, Bodmin and King's Lynn

'I pressed down on the mental accelerator. The old
lemon throbbed fiercely. I got an idea.'

P G Wodehouse

Contents

Acknowledgements

The content of this book includes contributions from many people, including myself. I have never felt it very useful to repackage something that works well simply to try to make it appear original. I much prefer to bring together elements that I believe create a useful collection of ideas and attribute these to the authors.

I want to thank all those who have contributed to Synectics over the years. George Prince and Bill Gordon who began it all 42 years ago made some wonderful insights into the nature of creativity, and many people over the years have built on this original research. (To find out more about Synectics Body of Knowledge go to www.synecticsworld.com.)

I also want to acknowledge the many people who have contributed to Neuro-Linguistic Programming (NLP). In particular, I thank Robert Dilts, who has allowed me to include his work on logical levels and the leadership model that uses these ideas. I also thank Julian Russell of Pace Personal Development Consulting for allowing me to use his personal mission and vision format. John Grinder and Richard Bandler are the George and Bill of NLP, who began the body of knowledge.

I thank Ben Fuchs for allowing the use of his work on conflict facilitation.

Claire Hewitt, once a client and now a colleague, gave me the story of human doing and human being. Caroline Flexman, a former colleague, pulled together a lot of the NLP material for some of the programmes we run in Synectics, and I have used this work freely. Between us, Caroline and I have worked with Pace Personal Development, John Seymour Associates and ITS on our paths to mastery and, inevitably, some of what we heard and saw is woven into this book. For myself, I would particularly like to acknowledge the insights I gained from Judith Lowe and Judith de Lozier in addition to those already mentioned.

My intention is to include in this book words and ideas with the permission of the originators, and I have asked several people to review the content to check this is so. If I have failed to ask anyone who feels he or she should have been consulted, please write to me through the publisher and let me know. In Synectics, the ownership of intellectual property is very clear, so I have little concern. In NLP, the ownership of ideas is much less clear, so I apologize to anyone who feels he or she has been missed. If you would like to check the origins of the NLP ideas, log on to www.NLPU.com. You will already know about positive intention if you are out there, so I hope you will accept mine. Future editions will be modified when we have spoken together.

Finally, thank you to Shannon Lee for dealing with the text and preparing the files to send to the publisher, Caroline Holt for proof-reading and Megan Hawthorn, Shannon and Sally Oakley for their work on the diagrams.

Introduction

I was talking with a colleague recently. She said that one of the moments in her life that she will always recall was when a friend said to her, 'The trouble with you is you are **a human doing, not a human being.**' This really made her sit up. She has a successful career, and life outside work is also good. She is very capable, yet she realized she was so busy **doing** that she never had time to **be.** Now she has both, and life is even better.

If I had £1 for every time someone in a business has said to me something like, 'The trouble is, we are all so busy **doing** things, we never have time to **think**; therefore we never **do** anything differently', I would be a rich man.

Doing is a vital part of life. Without **doing**, nothing ever happens. **Being** is a vital part of life. Without **being**, you will not use much of your potential **to do** in different ways.

George Prince, co-founder of Synectics, said, 'Everybody has a 1,000-horsepower mind; the trouble is they only use about 1 horsepower.'

So, life can be defined as **do be do be do be do…** Or, if you prefer – **do be do do, do be, do be do do…** You choose the tune, the rhythm, the tempo etc. Being able to play lots of tunes, therefore being flexible, is more likely to mean being a great person and maybe a great leader.

People with only one choice are robots.

I was speaking with someone who has responsibility for helping to release the talents and passions of the people in a large company.

This person argued that releasing passion in people and encouraging creativity was all but impossible because the Board kept changing. As a result, the rest of the firm was in a permanent state of flux and could see no point in becoming passionate in anything to do with work.

My view is that the world is a messy place and the way to survive is to notice what is happening and respond to this in the best way you can. Those who have the strongest sense of self, personal leadership, mastery of the tools of the trade, creativity and problem-solving skills will be most flexible and most successful. For a business to flourish, the Board needs to ensure its people are equipped to survive. If the Board provides an environment to encourage this, people will become passionate; if not, people will perform poorly or leave. That is up to the Board. This book contains the tools for survival.

I coined the word '**not-a-book**' to describe my first book, *Innovation and Creativity* (Kogan Page, 1995). This thing you hold in your hand has many book-like qualities – paper, words, diagrams – and if you simply read it, you will gain only a small percentage of what is available to you. Use it as a guide and reference on a path to mastery and you may never stop learning.

This book is about creativity, innovation and the leadership qualities that allow the possibility for this to flourish within you. It is also a guide for helping you to help others to flourish. This book is about **being** and **doing**. It offers a set of tools to explore **being**, leadership. It offers a series of tools for **doing**, creative problem solving and collaborative working. The tools are taken from my own experience working with Synectics and Neuro-Linguistic Programming. If you wish to read more about the background to these areas, see Appendices 3 and 4.

Human beings often put a lot of energy into many aspects of their life. They focus on achieving high levels of capabilities and skill over a range of interests. This book is more than words; it is images and has a tactile quality. In designing your life, I hope you will enjoy the many qualities you can bring to how you make sense of the world.

If you simply read the book and **do not do**, particularly **doing** the **being** bit, then you will get less from these pages.

Enjoy your journey, have some fun, do not be afraid of yourself – you are a powerful being; we all are!

The structure of this book

The book is laid out as follows:

- some thoughts on how to introduce creativity, innovation and change into a business – describing an ideal;

- a perspective about the world we live in from a creativity point of view;

- a map for **being** and **doing** in a business – living innovation;

- some things to **do** so that you can **be** – leadership for creativity;

- some things to **do** so that you can **do** – tools and techniques for creative problem solving;

- some suggestions for structures for working with groups, using common language and ways of organizing to maximize the probability of successful creativity.

If you want to read about **doing** before **being**, please feel free to do so.

Begin by testing your IQ (Innovation Quotient)

In Appendix 6 you will find a short series of questions designed to help you identify your current IQ. You may find it interesting to complete this before working with the material in the not-a-book, and then take the test again at the end and notice what has changed for you.

If you find you are already perfect you can always see if the shop will give you your money back. Alternatively you have one fewer Christmas present to buy.

Enjoy!!!!!!!!!

Some thoughts on how to introduce creativity, innovation and change into a business – describing an ideal

Introducing enduring creativity, innovation and change into an organization is about **beginning a journey**. Ideally, there is a **consistent map** that allows people to navigate on this journey, and there needs to be the **flexibility** for people to deal with the varying territory that they will have to cross.

Creativity, innovation and change begin with the top team if possible, ie the leadership group. All individuals in that team need to get clarity about their own beliefs and values and the role they wish to play in life, be it work life or home life.

Behaviours need to align with those personal values and beliefs; otherwise you can't function as a human being. (Actually you will, but probably in a very stressed way and at a lower level of performance than you might otherwise.) In business, behaviours need to model personal values and beliefs consistently; otherwise the other people in the organization will simply get confused, and low levels of trust will be created.

(For example, this was heard in one event I was facilitating: 'It is important to me that once a commitment is given the promise is kept. Someone who makes a commitment and lets me down will not be trusted in any context until they have acknowledged the slight and resolved the issue with me in person.')

Communication strategies such as mission statements, vision statements and statements of values form an important part of this process. However, they are only labels and as such are superficial. The important part of these statements is **how they are represented inside people's minds**. The top team's representations of those messages will be **communicated through behaviour**.

Once the senior team has completed this initial task of establishing their own sense of themselves, and modelling this in the context of the business, the journey rolls on to the next layer.

The next layer in the business needs to do the same piece of work, identifying with clarity their own beliefs and values and the behaviours that support these. This will be done in the context of their home life and the business, and in the context of the messages being delivered from the leadership team. This is why it is key that the leadership team models appropriate behaviour consistently; otherwise people cannot know what is appropriate and what is not appropriate.

Everyone in the next layer will identify **their** way of making the values of the business real, and it will be communicated through their behaviour. Because the sense of understanding of what the business and its values are about will be very deep and internal to each person, it means that individuals can have flexibility to communicate messages differently. However, these differences will all be aligned within a core context of business values.

Once the task has been completed for this layer, the journey rolls on another stage. The next layer also need to identify their own values and beliefs and how these align with the corporate ones. They also need to generate behaviours that are consistent with the corporate set of values that have been determined by the leadership team and are consistent with themselves as individuals.

In this way, the journey will generate a population of people who are aligned within themselves and can therefore function as human beings, and are aligned with the corporate set of values. This means that people can operate as individuals so that the firm benefits from the richness of having a diverse group of people.

The leadership team can have confidence that people will be working in a common way yet with flexibility so that, instead of

robots, you have heroes and heroines who can use their talents and latent capabilities.

People who find their individual values and beliefs cannot align with the corporate set will tend to leave the business.

This journey never ends and the role of the leaders is to model consistently what is appropriate for the business world of today and to be very clear when they are making changes, as they will have to, and clearly identify and communicate these through the business.

And when the world is less than ideal...?

Often businesses and the people in them change so fast there is no time to follow the ideal path. Most large change programmes fail because, even if the original plan was right, the world will have moved on by the time it is implemented and it is now wrong for the new market.

The ideal still remains useful as a guide to how to respond. If you know the people in your business will be likely to remain stable over time, life is easier. If you know it is likely you will get four MDs in three years (I know a business that did), then you have to be very flexible and fleet of foot in responding to the world in order to survive.

A sense of purpose and mission remains valid; you simply have to acknowledge it changes very quickly. The choice is to work with it or go somewhere else.

A perspective about the world we live in from a creativity point of view

The role of the leader is to establish conditions where flexibility and responsiveness thrive.

Successful companies are the ones that are able to respond flexibly to the world and remain competitive, because entrepreneurial flair and innovation are the lifeblood of the business.

The model that is described here addresses the many aspects of structure and behaviour that should be considered in order to make this a reality – **providing the vitality for health and growth in both individuals and the firm.**

Research into creativity, innovation and change in the USA, UK and Europe has consistently reported that 80 per cent of organizations feel innovation is vital to the business yet only about 4 per cent think they know how to do it. The actual statistics vary a little but not by much.

Organizations that succeed at managing creativity, innovation and change do the following very well:

- foster improved teamwork and communication;

- institute formal innovation programmes or expand existing ones;

- make meetings more productive;

- seek ideas from outside sources;

- understand the future needs of consumers/customers.

The research confirms a paradox that we have recognized for some time in Synectics. **It is process structure that allows the freedom to be creative** and to invent new ways of working, hence structured creative problem-solving processes and formal innovation programmes. Given total freedom, people do not know what to do or how to navigate through the confusion of new ideas and new thinking. **The frameworks and maps that are used for the journey need to release energy and encourage entrepreneurialism, not stifle it.**

Responsiveness and survival

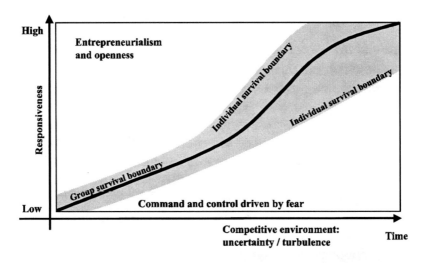

The black curved line in the diagram represents the stability curve for an organization. For an organization to remain healthy and competitive, it needs to be responsive to the external world and produce goods or services that the customer will buy. As the world moves on, which is represented by a right shift on the bottom axis, the firm needs to respond to the changes in order to move along the survival curve. Organizations that operate with command and control tend to maintain existing systems despite the world moving on, and end up below their curve and in trouble. An example in the recent past would be IBM's reluctance to let go of mainframe computers and start selling PCs as well. In the UK, the gap between the main supermarkets has opened up enormously. The losers are the ones that failed to respond to the changing world. Also, in retailing in the USA, Wal-Mart has stepped way out in front of traditional leading firms like Sears.

In the marketplace, firms that notice the world is moving on need to respond to this by finding a way of relinquishing what have become redundant command and control processes, in order to allow enterpreneurialism to flourish. This is not to overcriticize the original control processes. Often they were right at the time, and it is important to know when they are past their useful life.

The shaded area either side of the firm's survival curve represents individuals who work in the business. Individuals have an instant capacity to stretch and make changes if they choose to because they can operate faster than a corporate structure or set of rules may allow. Your corporate heroes and heroines, ie those people who actively seek to challenge today's way of working and may sometimes be regarded as a nuisance as they won't do as they are told, are crucial to maintaining the vitality of the firm.

The challenge for the leader is to run the operational world, designed to maintain business performance as it is today, and to allow people to move into the innovation world as well, so that they can operate flexibly and step outside of today's rules and structures in order to develop new ways of working. People who are **being** are important in both worlds; innovation is impossible without **being**.

Cycling worlds

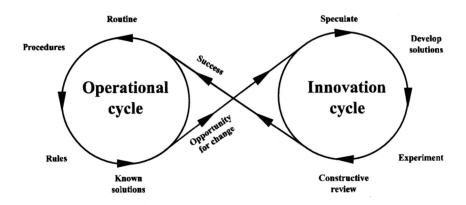

The cycling worlds model describes these two completely different cycles of behaviour, which represent different versions of the world. **Both worlds are important.**

The challenge for leaders is to maintain supportive and entrepreneurial climates in the operational world in order to maintain the business of today, and to help people build and use their skills and capabilities to be creative and innovative in order to create the business of tomorrow. **These worlds need to be managed simultaneously; however, it is impossible to be in them simultaneously.**

Leaders need to **identify the right people to do the right job. This means finding appropriate people for different contexts and giving people the capacity to be flexible** and to make different choices, depending upon which world they are operating in. A concept that may be helpful is to **treat information as useful or less useful, rather than right or wrong.**

In order to generate new behaviours and ways of working, businesses need a stream of ideas that lead to action and, as you will read later, a creative problem-solving structure to help them do this.

From ideas to action

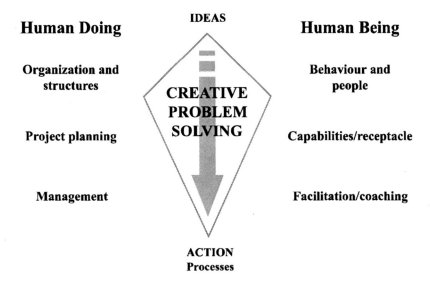

The classic approach in recent years to managing changes in businesses has been a structured approach, relying on project management in order to control the process of reorganizing the firm. Programmes that epitomize this are business process re-engineering, total quality and continuous improvement.

These approaches rely on a relatively simple model of the business as a means of communicating to employees how they fit. Providing people operate within the context of the model, results should be obtained. The trouble is the world is more complicated than the model. It is also full of people who do not fit the mould.

While most of these programmes have obtained some useful results, there have also been a lot of disappointments, and they have frequently had a de-energizing effect on the business. This is because structure is only half of the story. **Change only happens when people behave differently.**

In the short run, you may be able to get people to change just by telling them to do things differently. However, **in the long run, you will only get consistent change when new ways of working align**

with personal beliefs and values. Structures do not address these issues.

The organization can be regarded as a receptacle for its people. The analogy might be that of taking a newborn baby and nurturing it in your arms. This is necessary to help it grow and to develop skills and capabilities to help it to survive. It needs help and support.

People in the firm are no different. An organization that nurtures its people will release the potential and capability of them to excel. I mention George Prince's quote again, **'Everybody has a 1,000-horsepower mind; the trouble is they only use about 1 horsepower.'** Ask yourself the question, 'How many people do I know in my company who are run-of-the-mill performers at work yet outside excel in other activities like amateur sports, charity events etc?'

The following diagram describes the pay-off when you focus on producing a cooperative and supportive climate in your business.

Creating the field and climate

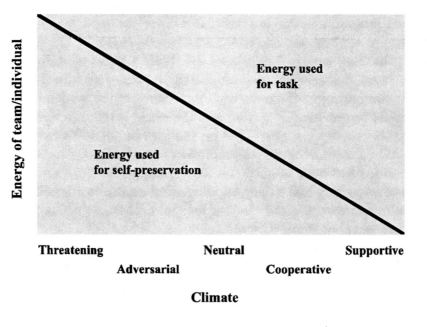

Where a business operates in a climate of fear and people feel threatened, then their energy will be focused on self-protection. This will sap vitality from the organization. It might feel like too much effort to face the challenges that arise, so people stop bothering. Motivation is lost, and managers often revert to command and control, which destroys any new behaviour and builds a downward spiral towards final dictatorship.

An organization that can operate so that the people feel supported releases energy for entrepreneurialism, creativity and focus on task and success.

Major international snack foods company saves £100,000 through better meeting management

One of the world's largest snack foods companies used Synectics to halve their meeting time while at the same time increasing their effectiveness. The company had been running their meetings out of habit, stuck in a routine of diarized four-weekly sessions. Little ownership existed and consequently people generally left meetings with more of a sense of let-down than optimism.

The division leader felt that meetings were particularly important in his sales group, where individual team members don't work together frequently. He and his team were determined to improve the effectiveness of their meetings, not only to make better use of time but also to increase creativity and build morale. They consequently embarked on Synectics training.

At times, it wasn't easy for the client team and they had to make several steps backwards in 'relearning' their meeting process before really making consistent improvements. Probably the most critical factor in their success was going in with eyes open and acknowledging that substantive change takes time, effort and persistence. Over a number of months, the team made some dramatic steps forward.

By ensuring the right agenda items were scheduled, clear ownership and objectives tabled for each and adequate time allocated, team members now look forward to the meetings as a value-add and not a drag.

'We have reduced the amount of meeting time by 50 per cent (worth around £100,000 in released time) and yet have improved the quality of output significantly.'

Commercial Development Director

International airport operator doubles retail income through climate of innovation

International airport operator used Synectics to double their retail income after their retail board had articulated the main strategies and objectives. The retail team needed to work out how to achieve them and Synectics was called in to assist with the project.

One hundred and twenty managers on the retail team were facilitated by Synectics in one large workshop-style conference, using Synectics innovation tools and techniques to create a tactical programme of new ideas to fulfil the vision. This involved everyone thinking outside their usual boundaries, contributing to areas they would not normally be involved with. The groups created a new organization structure to support what they needed to do and generated implementable action plans out of the new ideas. The board made vital decisions throughout the three days, as people came up with exciting new plans.

There was total commitment and 'buy-in' from everyone concerned because they were creating their own future. Participants learnt new empowering skills and evolved a 'can do' way of working that released each other's abilities and energy. The effect continued long after the event.

Against an initial target of two years, the operator doubled its retail income in 18 months. The success of this energized, go-ahead cultural style was held up as a model for other divisions, while the retail team carried the innovation tools and techniques into everyday working life and lived in a working atmosphere of consistent innovation.

'I found working with Synectics extremely useful in using various creative thinking approaches in a practical focused way that enabled ideas to be properly developed and implemented, instead of being left in the air.'

Management Development Manager

A map for *being* and *doing* in a business – living innovation

The big picture – the map for navigating on the journey

Enterprise Innovation

Growing the business and learning

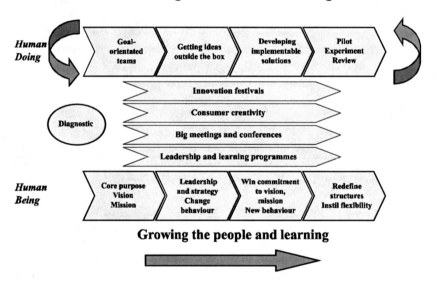

Growing the people and learning

The map labels the activities in which you may engage on your journey.

The **Human Doing** stream is about **doing**. It represents structured approaches to **creative problem solving** and **tools and techniques** to make them really effective. This includes establishing clear ownership of problems, getting ideas and developing solutions.

The **Human Being** stream is about **being**. It represents working on beliefs and values so that the people and culture of your firm are aligned with the business goals, and the focus on business performance is maintained throughout the journey.

The linking activities that provide energy for these streams to flourish are indicated by the diagnostic ellipse and the four streams of activity, innovation festivals, etc.

Bringing **being** and **doing** together

The two streams can be managed separately or in parallel. The book contains the tools for learning skills and capabilities for each stream. Some clues about some typical ways to provide energy and direction to the streams in addition to specifically focusing on the tools and techniques are:

▓ **Diagnostic**

Find ways to explore and monitor the ways energy is being used in your organization. Discover the capabilities and preferences for behaviour of your people and harness this for the benefit of the organization. My own preferred tool is Insights® Profiling to give you one example; see www.insightsworld.com.

▓ **Innovation festivals**

Get people together in order to explore issues, develop ideas and create solutions. Make them special and often; keep the audience broad; find interesting places to hold them.

▓ **Consumer creativity**

Involve your customers and consumers directly in helping you to invent strategy, products and services. Bring them into your business and work with them problem solving and creating new solutions. They are not hampered by your own corporate beliefs about possibility and they speak the language of the street.

■ **Big meetings and conferences**

Bring together large groups in your firm and use the processes and structures you will read about in the book to involve hundreds at a time in exploring and feeding back opinions about the firm – a great way to win commitment and release boundless energy into the organization.

■ **Leadership and learning programmes**

Spend time, energy and money developing your people at all levels. Leadership refers to hierarchy and to taking control of your own life so it is appropriate for people at all levels; you will simply modify your approach to suit. Committed skilled people will make 2 + 2 = at least 5!

The following part of the book invites you to explore **being,** and then we will take a look at **doing**.

This part of the book is about

Being

*Some things to **Do** so that you can **Be** – leadership for creativity*

When exploring **being**, it can be helpful to operate in your mind as though certain presuppositions about the world are true. What follows are not '**truths**'; however, if you operate as though they are, you are more likely to have a fruitful exploration of **being**.

I use the expression 'the system' in the following pages. Sometimes this refers to the individual and what is going on inside; sometimes it refers to groups and organizations, in which case the focus is on the outside. If this sounds rather cryptic, go with the flow and read on for a while. 'Stay loose until rigour counts' is one of the ground rules for creative meetings. Become comfortable with some approximate thinking for a while until clarity presents itself; your mind is a great tool for doing (**being**) this.

As you read the following pages about the nature of subjective experience, you may like to consider a series of scenarios or contexts that you are experiencing right now. The following diagram on the nature of subjective experience represents a series of labels that can be attached to ways we try to make sense of the world.

Notice what comes to mind as you consider these scenarios in the context of each of the labels.

This diagram shows how we create our realities using information from outside – **sight, sound, smell** etc. We filter this experience and seek to fit our experiences to existing **maps**. The maps represent the way we **programmed** a previous experience, and this allows us to make instant decisions when faced with another set of inputs that are similar. For example, if I ask you for a glass of water, I stand a good chance of getting this, rather than a teddy bear, because most of us have a common experience and map that represents a glass of water. Even at this simple level, we may have a problem – do I mean still or sparkling?

Also, we are chemical systems and have **feelings** that relate to our maps. For example, if you saw a dog snarling at you, frothing at the mouth, I imagine you have a programme that results in a **feeling** you might describe as **fear** or **nervousness**.

Based upon this feeling, you will behave in some way that influences the world, the world changes and so the cycle continues.

Flexible people have more maps. Creativity is about remaining curious and exploring meaning from new experiences about the world rather than assuming it just fits a previous experience. It amazes me when I am working on new product development and other marketing projects how often my clients want to fit the data into categories or themes in order to make things tidy and promote understanding. These themes rarely represent any real version of the world that you will ever find; however, they are convenient. Creativity is about observing, exploring, noticing and responding, not about making instant assumptions that you know.

The nature of subjective experience

This is about how we as individuals experience the world and make sense of that experience. The following is an explanation of what this term means and includes a set of ideas described using the same language you will find if you choose to read other books about NLP. Also see Appendix 4, which describes the origins of NLP.

The map is not the territory

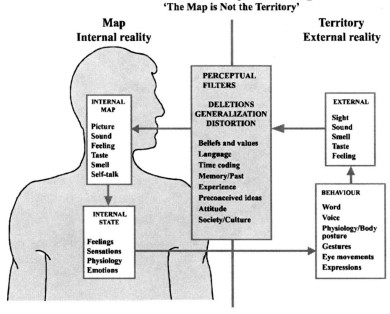

The nature of subjective experience
'The Map is Not the Territory'

Map Internal reality		Territory External reality
INTERNAL MAP	PERCEPTUAL FILTERS	EXTERNAL
Picture Sound Feeling Taste Smell Self-talk	DELETIONS GENERALIZATION DISTORTION	Sight Sound Smell Taste Feeling
	Beliefs and values Language Time coding Memory/Past Experience Preconceived ideas Attitude Society/Culture	
INTERNAL STATE		BEHAVIOUR
Feelings Sensations Physiology Emotions		Word Voice Physiology/Body posture Gestures Eye movements Expressions

▨ People have their own unique map of the world based on their perception of reality and past experiences.

▨ No individual map of the world is any more **real** or **true** than any other.

▨ People respond to their own perceptions of reality or map of the world.

▨ The meaning of my communication to another person is the response it elicits in that person regardless of my intention.

▨ People make choices and decisions based on their unique map of the world. Any behaviour, no matter how strange or unhelpful, is the best choice available to a person given his or her perceived map of the world at that point in time.

▨ The '**wisest**' maps are those that make available the widest and richest number of choices, as opposed to being the most 'real' or 'accurate'.

▨ People already have (or potentially have) all the internal resources they need to act effectively. As Walt Disney said, 'If you can dream it, you can do it.'

▨ Creativity and change come from enriching a person's map of the world by releasing an appropriate resource or activating a potential resource, ie by giving the person more choices.

Life and mind are systemic processes

▨ Life and mind include many systems and subsystems that interact and mutually influence each other, eg:
- mind/body;
- conscious/unconscious;
- person/person;
- person/society;
- society/society;
- etc.

▓ You cannot not influence; you cannot not communicate. (Think about it: the very act of trying not to do either of these means you just did.)

▓ It is not possible completely to isolate any part of a system from the rest of the system. Interactions between people form feedback loops – people will be affected by the results that their own actions have on other people.

▓ There are no failures, only feedback. Feedback gives us the opportunity to learn and do something different if appropriate. I often get challenged on this one. Remember, we are dealing with presumptions, not **truths**. There are contexts where there are failures. When a machine breaks, it fails. Here I am saying that treating an experience as feedback keeps you in a mindset that stays open to learning. Failure often leads to giving up or assuming the other party was wrong.

Edison experimented with 6,000 substances when seeking a material that could be used for light bulb filaments. He regarded every 'failed' experiment as one less material to try as he worked his way towards a solution.

▓ Any behaviour has or had a positive intention in some context. A behaviour may be a resource or limitation, depending on how it fits in with the rest of the system. The positive intention is for the person behaving, not necessarily towards you. Muggers will have a positive intention for them, not necessarily towards you. I still suggest you run like hell if approached by a mugger. Understanding the positive intention may be useful later to give you other choices about how to behave.

▓ Not all interactions in a system are on the same level. It is useful to separate behaviour from 'self' – to separate the positive intent or belief that generated the behaviour from the behaviour itself.

The law of requisite variety

▓ As environments and contexts change, our actions will not always produce the same result. A minimum amount of flexibility is required in order to adapt and survive within a system.

▓ The amount of flexibility required will depend on the complexity and variability/uncertainty in the system. As a system becomes more complex, more flexibility is required.

▓ The people with the most flexibility have the highest probability of achieving the results they want. The part of the system that has the greatest variety of possible responses will be the controlling element.

▓ If what you are doing is not getting the response you want, then keep varying your own behaviour until you do.

'Deep structure' and 'surface structure'

▓ Language is a very imprecise tool. Expressions, actions and reactions are surface structures, which are the result of an attempt to convey the meaning of a deeper structure. Different surface structures may be reflections of a common deep structure.

▓ The transformation from deep structure into surface structure often results in information being generalized, distorted or deleted. Many examples of surface structures may be required in order to convey an understanding of a deeper structure, eg 'We are going to behave in a customer-focused way.' Imagine how many meanings that may have and the scope for argument that exists. Customer focus is a deep-structure concept that will require many surface-level examples in order to become useful in a business.

▓ There are multiple levels of successively deeper structures in the structure and organization of systems. All levels of a

Words, actions, pictures, metaphors and symbols

Expressions, applications and content

SURFACE STRUCTURE

DELETIONS

GENERALIZATIONS

DISTORTIONS

DEEP STRUCTURE

Principles, concepts and processes

Ideas, experiences and emotions

system's structure should be addressed in order to achieve ecological change, eg producing a new organizational chart is meaningless unless you also deal with the people who are a part of the organization.

The concept of deep and surface structure is useful when thinking about company mission and vision statements. I wrote earlier that these statements are important; however, they are only superficial labels and what really matters is what is in the minds that generate a statement, and the behaviours that support it.

Now you can understand why. The statement will have one meaning for the person who created it, and different meanings for everyone else because they have different experience.

Leadership style and logical levels of influence and change

You are going to play with a concept called 'logical levels' as a way of exploring **being**. Logical levels also can be used to describe different leadership styles and how they relate to creativity and innovation. What follows gives an overview of this, and we return to it later after you have run some more experiments with **being**.

The table is a logical levels framework developed by Robert Dilts.

Environment	Creating a context	**Constraints and opportunities**	Where? When?
Behaviours	Influencing people's bodies	**Actions and reactions** taken within the environment	What?
Capabilities	Strategies and states (emotional resources) – influencing people's minds	Give **direction** to behavioural actions through a **mental map, plan or strategy**	How?
Beliefs and values	Meanings and what's important – influencing people's behaviour	Provide the reinforcement, **permission and motivation** that support or deny capabilities	Why? What's important?
Identity	Sense of self	Determine overall purpose, **mission**	Who?
Spirit	The larger system – family, community, organization and global systems	**Vision and purpose**	Who else?

The movement from Environment to Spirit is analogous to moving from surface to deep structure.

When seeking to get more creativity and innovation into an organization, it is important to have an understanding of the different levels of influence and at what level you are operating. The language that people use and the emphasis that they put on certain words reflect these different levels.

The emphasis on different parts of a sentence can cover all different logical levels:

Identity	*You* can't do that here.
Belief	You *can't* do that here.
Capability	You can't *do* that here.
Behaviour	You can't do *that* here.
Environment	You can't do that *here*.

It is often important to identify and separate at which level you wish to communicate with someone. For example, when giving feedback on unacceptable behaviour, it is important to keep your feedback at the level of behaviour rather than identity (which may feel like an attack on the person's sense of self). See Appendix 2 on conflict facilitation for a model that relates to this experience.

Types of leadership

Meta-leadership – big picture

▨ Creating a vision of the future.

▨ Giving people a sense of purpose in what they and the organization are doing.

▨ Linking individuals through that vision to their environment, releasing energy and enthusiasm.

Macro-leadership – strategy and plans

▨ Creating a successful organization through path finding and culture building.

▨ Path finding – finding the way to a successful future.

▨ Culture building – drawing people into a purposeful organization and building commitment.

▨ Linking individuals to the organization.

Micro-leadership – day-to-day tasks and actions

▨ Managing tasks – directing people in the accomplishment of specific tasks.

▨ Managing relationships – creating an efficient working atmosphere.

▨ Obtaining willing cooperation in getting the job done by adjusting one's leadership style – balancing task and relationship behaviour.

Take a moment to consider these different levels of leadership and think about which ones are more likely to release creative potential both in yourself and in others. Remind yourself of the most recent leadership decisions you made and now reflect upon whether you used the most useful approach; or maybe you now see how a different choice might have elicited a more useful response.

Types of leadership skills

Self skills	▓ Managing your self and your thinking patterns
	▓ Managing your emotional states
Relational skills (with others)	▓ Influencing
	▓ Understanding
	▓ Motivating
	▓ Communicating
Strategic thinking skills	▓ Defining and achieving specific goals and objectives
Systemic thinking skills	▓ Identifying and understanding the larger system in which you are operating, ie department, organization, industry, market place, etc
	▓ Managing complexity and uncertainty

Take a walk up the levels

This is an exercise both mental and physical. It will be different depending upon whether or not you sit in a chair or stand up and walk around whatever space you are in. Exploring **being** will be a different experience if you get up, move around and then notice the different perspectives from different physical spaces. I recommend you stand up.

This is an exercise in sorting life out. Most of us go through life just doing things and if the question were asked of you, 'How do you do that?', you could not give an answer. Ask the same question of an Olympic athlete and the athlete will know exactly how he or she does it. Performance coaching is about learning how you do things, focusing on the detail and raising performance. For the exercise that follows, it is important to answer the specific questions and to differentiate between the various bits of information.

Begin by writing each of the logical levels on to two pieces of paper and placing these on the floor in order, beginning with **Environment**. Place the two sets in parallel (see the diagram on the following page). You now have two sets of tiles to walk on. Nominate one as the **present state** and the other as a **desired state**. You can do the following on your own, or work with someone you trust who can write down the information for you as you experience the journey:

1. Choose an area of your life that you would like to explore, where you would like to be more creative. (It may be a particular meeting you attend, a project you have or a colleague you always respond to in a certain way that leaves you feeling bad, either about him or her or about yourself.)

2. Walk through the logical levels step by step in the **present** state. Do this by stepping on to each tile in turn. You may find it helpful to close your eyes. As you stop at each level and consider what comes to mind, notice what you **see**, **hear** and **feel** in that place. Take as long as you like to do this. As you finish, you may wish to make some notes of what came to mind. Ask yourself the question that relates to each level repeatedly – see the following diagram – to help gather the information. Make sure you answer the specific question on the level, not another one.

3. Walk through the logical levels step by step in the **desired state**. Again, follow the same process as in step 2.

4. Now, step away from the tiles and take a look at what you have discovered. Notice where in the present state seems to feel the 'right place' to give attention to, ie where does it feel wrong? Trust your intuition in **doing (being)** this.

5. Assign the label **role identity** to this 'right place'. Step on to the tiles in the **present state** and experience again what you **see**, **hear** and **feel**.

6. Step across to the **desired state** and notice the differences between the **present** and **desired** states. Let your mind develop a rich picture of what life will be like when you really have the **desired state**. You may care to walk up and down the

logical levels as you do this. Stay focused on the different pieces of information that apply to the different logical levels. It is this specificity that can more easily help you identify specific changes you may choose to make.

7. Carry all this knowledge back to now by walking to the **environment** in the **present state** and look back into the future.

8. Step away and finish. You may choose to make notes about what you will **do** differently as a result of **being**.

You will have an opportunity to revisit this journey later. I will suggest ways to fine-tune your experiences as you read through this part of the book and experience **being**.

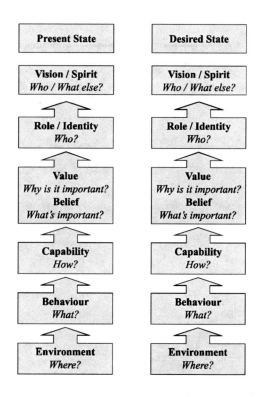

Mission and Vision

If you don't know where you are going,

how will you know when you get there?

'... when she was a little startled by seeing the Cheshire Cat sitting on a bough of a tree a few yards off.

The Cat only grinned when it saw Alice. It looked good-natured, she thought: still it had very long claws and a great many teeth, so she felt that it ought to be treated with respect.

"Cheshire Puss," she began, rather timidly, as she did not at all know whether it would like the name: however, it only grinned a little wider. "Come, it's pleased so far," thought Alice, and she went on. "Would you tell me, please, which way I ought to go from here?"

"That depends a good deal on where you want to get to," said the Cat.

"I don't much care where–" said Alice.

"Then it doesn't matter which way you go," said the Cat.

"–so long as I get somewhere," Alice added as an explanation.

"Oh, you're sure to do that," said the Cat, "if you only walk long enough."'

Lewis Carroll, *Alice's Adventures in Wonderland*

What could you achieve that would really mean that you fulfil your dreams?

Exploring your mission and vision is designed to open up new realms of possibility that enable you to answer this question for yourself, and to move on to a path of personal and professional excellence, on a journey to mastery.

The purpose of what follows is to enable you to express your mission more clearly on a day-to-day basis and to plan your future clearly based on this sense of mission.

It is within the context of your individual mission in life that you can really be motivated, and understanding how aligning your personal beliefs and values with this mission is what will help you perform as a leader.

Mission

How you fulfil your purpose in life so that, having lived to your utmost, you feel satisfied at the end of your life. The clearer we are about our personal mission, the more we can apply it on a daily basis in a practical way.

People who are implementing their mission to their satisfaction are motivated, inspired, creative, hard-working, playful and effective. Your mission is not an end result so much as a direction in which there is always room for enhancement and fine-tuning. Missions are not necessarily fixed, though they often remain the same for decades. A person who is going through a life transition is often 're-missioning'.

Vision

The end result that you personally are seeking to create. 'Vision' tends to focus you on medium- or long-term outcomes, rather than short-term goals and objectives.

Your vision is your target. Your mission is the quality you bring to the journey.

Some people already know their mission without having the resources or the courage in place to implement it. Although missions can be expressed in every activity we do on a daily basis, some jobs give more room for its individual expression than others.

For example, I often find myself listening to leaders who describe a rich picture of how they wish their company to be and what people will be doing. However, they claim to be frustrated because it is not happening and they do not know what to do. Often these same leaders are feared by the organization because they resort to telling people repeatedly what they want, yet they never behave in a way that supports this.

> **Do not fear your power, nor be afraid to be and live your mission, because only then will you lose your fear of yourself.**
>
> *Jonne Ceserani*

Chunking up three outcomes to find your personal mission

'Chunking' is an expression that describes ways of looking at anything in different-size lumps. You will have heard the old joke, 'How do you eat an elephant?' Answer, 'One bite at a time.' This is chunking. Later you will have a chance to chunk down and sideways, but for now you are simply going to chunk up.

As before, you can do this on your own, though it can be more rewarding to work with someone you trust:

1. Choose three personal or job outcomes in three different contexts. Any combination of contexts is fine. My preference is to choose a mix of work, personal and a great dream you have for yourself. This means you can easily spot the similarities behind your purpose, across diverse contexts.

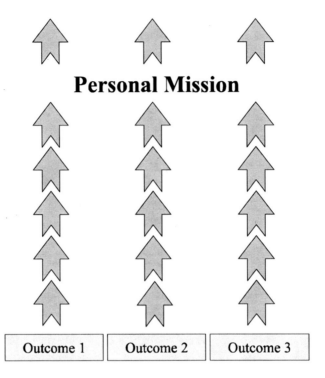

Personal Mission

| Outcome 1 | Outcome 2 | Outcome 3 |

- I want to achieve 25 per cent sales growth year on year for my company.
- I want to meet together with my partner and all my grown-up children at least twice a year in our home.
- I want to sail my own yacht across the Atlantic, with friends.

2. Now, take each outcome in turn and chunk it up, working through the logical levels. Begin by asking the specific question on each level that relates to that level, as you did earlier, eg Environment, 'Where am I when I am experiencing this?' (See diagram on page 35) Ask the same question several times for each level so that you collect as rich a picture as possible with lots of detail. Once you have this information, ask yourself either or both of the following questions about that information. The question/s to ask yourself each time are:

If I achieved this... what would it do for me?

And / or

What would… give me?

For example, the answer to 'Where am I?' might be 'In a conference centre, facing my sales team, including my bosses, with lights focused on me on a stage.'

In answering 'What would standing on a stage give me?', I might say 'A feeling of power', and what that would give me might be 'A feeling of humbleness', and what that would give me might be 'Serenity', and so on.

This is an exploration so there are no 'right' answers. You can choose to explore for as long as you find it interesting and useful. Not all the answers will come to you immediately because you are leaving behind surface structures and exploring deep structures. You do not need to complete the exercise in one go; you may return to it many times.

Do not be afraid of what you find. It is in you anyway, so look for how useful whatever you find can be in your life.

My own mission is **'Finding the wow in everything, even sadness.'** Of course, this only really has meaning for me and, as it is my mission, that is as it should be. In reaching this set of words as I chunked up, I found myself giving answers like, **'I will be a god.'** I use a lower case 'g' deliberately! The point is that, for me, **'god'** and **'respect'** have similar meaning. I also assign **'quality'** to **'god'** and this relates to 'wow' for me.

The exploration you are about to make goes into the deep structure. This means exploring your subconscious. Try to avoid censoring what comes to mind in terms of right and wrong in the world you currently live in. Welcome your **being** and enjoy what you find.

There is nothing good or bad, but thinking makes it so.

William Shakespeare

---

3. Mark the information in each column concerned with **skills/capability** issues, what you are **about,** and levels to do with **spiritual** issues, what it's all about for you.

4. Explore the levels in between, looking for common themes and ideas. Ask questions like: where in this list is what is most important to me? What is my uniqueness? Does this describe my purpose?

5. Find a set of words that expresses your mission or purpose in life. This exercise presupposes:

   – You will identify what is most important to your well-being.
   – At some point, you shift from wanting something on the outside to wanting a deep, inner, core-feeling state. Try not to concern yourself with **how** you will achieve the mission at this point because this can get in the way of acknowledging your mission.

Well formedness conditions for your mission statement:

– Stated in the positive.
– Outcome concerns process or direction, not results.
– Specified at appropriate level, ie 'above' job description and 'below' spiritual.
– Applies to self and others.

Some examples of mission statements:

– To make a difference.
– Realizing that anything is possible.
– To discover what my oak tree is.
– Belonging in the community, freedom to give.
– To encourage freedom in myself and others.
– Radiating brilliance.
– Enchantment.
– Love – the emotional freedom to grow.
– Facilitating being.
– Exploring the confidence to be relaxed and aware, while meeting challenge.
– … and many more.

Strategies for implementing your vision: realizing vision through a 500-year action plan

First create your **Vision**. Do this using the following exercise. Experience the exercise from your sense of **Mission** that you worked on earlier.

Timelines

Timelines are a 'pseudo-orientation in time' to describe experiences of looking on life from any time other than the present moment.

I invite you to explore timelines by imaginatively externalizing past, present and future as a 'line' or path on the floor in front of you. The timeline is just a metaphor and as such it may be helpful to remember that lines are as thick or as thin as you choose to make them. This spatial representation of time will not necessarily coincide with how you organize past, present and future in your mind's eye. For these memories, you may use a different metaphor altogether – cycles, spirals, landscapes, for example. However, you may find it convenient to adopt the method of spatially organizing time on the floor (or ground) in front of you as a timeline.

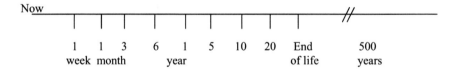

| | 1 week | 1 month | 3 | 6 | 1 year | 5 | 10 | 20 | End of life | 500 years |

1. Step on to your timeline 500 years in the future and **see**, **hear** and **feel** your vision of how you'd like the world to be, keeping your sense of mission in mind as you reflect upon this.

2. Walk back to the end of your life, where you ask yourself, 'What contribution can I make in my lifetime?'

3. Continue walking back to the present, asking yourself, 'What can I achieve – in 30 years? 20 years? 10 years? Forward to now?'

Moving towards your goal

This section crosses the boundary a little between **being** and **doing**. Now that you have explored **being**, this is an opportunity to identify some clear goals, comfortable in the knowledge that you have your sense of **being**. Following this is an opportunity to explore ways of fine-tuning **being** and how your internal map of the world is externalized through language, behaviour, etc.

The paradox of creativity, innovation and leadership is that if you are inventing something new you often don't know where you are going – it's like driving in the fog. The Synectics Creative Problem-Solving Process in the appendix on structures may help here, and the tools for this are in the **doing** section. They will help you navigate the fog. Knowing your desired outcome, and being precise about how you will know that you have achieved it, will allow you to measure whether you have arrived.

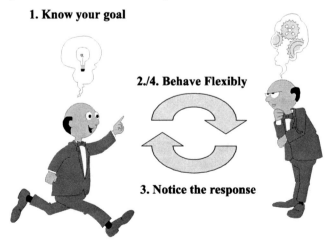

1. Know your goal

2./4. Behave Flexibly

3. Notice the response

It may sometimes be difficult to determine a specific goal, for example if you want to invent a new product. However, you can be specific about what that product might achieve for your organization or for your customers. In addition, you can specify the number of concepts you wish to invent, which can then be explored further.

Once you know your goal, you can experiment with ways of achieving it. If you pay attention to the results and responses you get to your actions, you can then check whether your actions are moving you closer to realizing your goal. If the effect of your actions is not what you want, you can then modify your actions.

> ■ **If what you're doing isn't working, do something different – anything, as long as it's different from what you were doing before.**
>
> ■ **There is no such thing as failure, only feedback.**

A definition of insanity is continuing to do the same thing and expecting a different result.

Defining the specifics of your task or goal

> *Be careful what you wish for (or think about) as you might just get it!*
>
> Anon

▓ **State your goal in the positive,** ie as a goal you can move towards. Your unconscious doesn't understand negatives and focuses on what you are thinking about (eg try **not** thinking of the colour blue).

▓ **Be specific about what you want** – use questions to uncover any vagueness:
  - **Who?**
  - **How?**
  - **What?**
  - **Where?**
  - **When?**

Avoid using Why? as this will uncover beliefs rather than specific information about the task.

▓ **Focus on the results you want** rather than the current state of affairs, ie:

outcomes	instead of	**problems;**
possibilities	instead of	**limitations;**
how?	instead of	**why?**
useful	instead of	**right or wrong.**

Chunking your task or goal to increase motivation

Is your task or goal in the appropriate bite-sized chunk?

> Q   *How do you eat an elephant?*
> A   *One bite at a time.*

▨ In setting goals or objectives, people often forget differences in thinking styles:
  - Some people prefer to think about large goals or the big picture, but when the time comes for action have no idea what to do.
  - Others are happier thinking about details and may be overwhelmed if a goal is too big.

▨ In addition, if a goal is too small, it may not provide the motivation to spur someone into action. In this case, it can become important to link the goal to a bigger or more important goal that someone is motivated towards.

Choose a task or goal, say 'How to promote creativity and innovation in the workplace':

1. **Is the task too big, vague or unspecific? – Chunk down.**
   Ask yourself, 'What is stopping me from…' (identifying the problem) or 'What do I want instead…?' (turn into a positive).

2. **Is the task too small to motivate me? – Chunk up.**
   Ask yourself, 'If I achieved this… what would it do for me?' or 'What would… give me?'

3. **Is the task one of a class of opportunities? – Chunk sideways.**
   Ask yourself, 'What's another example of that?' or 'What else might achieve the same result?' or 'What are the benefits?'

Increasing commitment to a task or goal

> *'Until one is fully committed, there is hesitancy, the chance to draw back, always ineffectiveness. Concerning all acts of initiative (and creation), there is one elementary truth, the ignorance of which kills countless ideas and splendid plans: that the moment one definitely commits oneself, then providence moves too.*
>
> *All sorts of things occur to help one that would never otherwise have occurred. A whole stream of events issues from the decision, raising in one's favour all manner of unforeseen incidents and meetings and material assistance, which no man could have dreamt would have come his way.*
>
> *Whatever you can do or dream you can, begin it.*
>
> *Boldness has genius, magic and power in it.*
>
> *Begin it now.'*
>
> Goethe

In order to follow through with goals and tasks, we need to be committed to them. One way of ensuring commitment is to look at a task from a number of different angles in order to ensure that we really want to do it – these are called the **conditions for a well-formed outcome**.

Any objections or concerns that are uncovered can be solved using the Synectics Creative Problem-Solving Process.

Conditions for a well-formed outcome

▩ **Positive** – what do you want?

▓ **Achievement** – how will you know you have succeeded?

▓ **Specific context** – in what context do you want this outcome?

▓ **Ownership** – can you start and maintain this outcome?

▓ **Resources** – who or what is available to help you?

▓ **Consequences** – if you could have it tomorrow, would you keep it?

▓ **Action plan and midpoint goals** – what is the next step?

Try taking an outcome that is important to you and respond to the statements and answer the questions that follow:

1. **Positive – what do you want?**
   State your goal/outcome in the positive – moving towards a desired goal and not away from something undesirable.
   – If stated in the negative, ask – what do you want instead?

2. **Achievement – how will you know you have succeeded?**
   – How will you know that you have achieved your outcome?
   – What will you be seeing, hearing and feeling? Get really specific.
   – How will someone else know that you have achieved your outcome?
   – What will that person be seeing you do and hearing you say? Again, get specific.

3. **Specific context – in what context do you want this outcome?**
   – When do you want it? When don't you want it?
   – With whom do you want it? With whom might it not be appropriate?
   – Where do you want it? In what situations might it not be appropriate?

4. **Ownership – can you start and maintain this outcome?**
   – What can you do directly to achieve your outcome?
   – What is under your control and what is not?

- If this is your goal for someone else or your department, what is your goal for your own behaviour or skills/capabilities within the situation?
- What can you do to persuade and influence others to help you?

5. **Resources – who or what is available to help you?**
   - What personal qualities and skills do you have to help you achieve your goal?
   - Who else might be able to help you?
   - What role models do you have – who has done this successfully before?
   - What other resources do you have?

6. **Consequences – if you could have it tomorrow, would you keep it?**
   - What will happen if you get your outcome?
   - How much time and effort will this outcome take?
   - Who else is affected and how will they feel about it?
   - What are the benefits of maintaining the status quo and doing nothing?
   - How can you keep the benefits of the present situation?
   - Is your outcome representative of who you are and where you want to be?
   - What will this outcome do for you if you achieve it?

7. **Action plan and midpoint goals – what is the next step?**
   - What roles will people play?
   - Who is responsible for the different actions?
   - When will the different actions be achieved by?
   - Who else needs to be involved, consulted or informed?
   - How does this fit in with other or larger outcomes?
   - Are there any smaller outcomes that need to be achieved in order to overcome obstacles?
   - What midpoint goals will let you know you are on track for achieving your overall outcome?

How is your outcome now and how is it changing? Maybe it is the same, and that is OK as well.

Accessing emotional resources and high-performance states

This is about how to recapture occasions from the past when you were working really well and feeling really good about yourself so that you can use this past experience to help you perform well in the present and the future.

You are now going to explore some fine-tuning mechanisms for **being**. To use a metaphor – if so far you have bulldozed the field, built some foundations and put up the basic structure of walls and ceilings, now you are painting the frescos.

Sub-modalities are the finer points, the detail of how we represent our inner experience in the outer world. You can think of sub-modalities as the fine-tuning knob on the television or the focusing button on a camera. For example, if I say, 'The light became increasingly brighter and more intense', the sub-modalities are brightness and intensity.

We will explore **representation systems** a little further on in the book but, before this, I think you will find it interesting to explore more of **being** using sub-modalities.

I will just touch on the **representation systems** briefly first. This is **a surface structure** concept. Notice the word, **re-present**. We use language to **re-present** our internal experience. A set of labels to describe the categories of representation is:

Visual	I see the way forward
Auditory	I can hear the final whistle about to blow
Kinaesthetic	I feel I know where I am going
Olfactory	I know we will come up smelling of roses
Gustatory	I found success very sweet

There is a category outside of this set – **internal dialogue** – when you are talking to yourself in your mind and processing thoughts, commonly called thinking.

Try this exercise to sample the effect of changing sub-modalities. Take some time over it; do not rush. You can do it by reading it to yourself. If you have someone to read it for you, it will be even more rewarding:

1. Close your eyes (you can leave them open while you are reading if you are doing this on your own) and imagine an event in your life in which you were extremely excited and enthusiastic about what you were doing. In your mind's eye, imagine stepping back into this event, reliving the experience as if you were having it all over again. Pay attention to the sights and sounds around you and the feelings you are experiencing as if the event were happening here and now.

2. Notice whether you are looking through your own eyes or whether you can see yourself in the picture. If you can see yourself in the picture, move towards your body and step into your shoes, experiencing the feelings of excitement and enthusiasm from inside your body, seeing the events through your own eyes.

3. As you are looking at the situation in your mind's eye, notice the qualities of the picture, the size, whether it is like a moving film or a still photograph, whether it is colour or black and white, whether it has a frame around it or anything else unusual that strikes you.

4. As you watch those images, pay close attention to the physical feelings that you may be experiencing in your body. If you were to give a name to the emotions attached to those feelings, what would it be? As you are experiencing all of those feelings, pay attention to just how intense those feelings are.

5. As you are looking at this image in your mind, imagine you have a brightness control knob next to the image, similar to the one on a television set. Knowing that you can always adjust the

brightness to its normal setting, imagine turning that knob slowly to a brighter image, stopping while the picture is still clearly definable.

6. Now, pay attention to your feelings and notice whether the feelings that go with that image have changed in any way. How have they changed now that your picture is brighter?

7. Now, turn down the brightness of the picture, again knowing that you can readjust the brightness later. Continue to turn it so that the image in your mind becomes so dim that you can barely see it.

8. Again, pay attention to your feelings as your experience of that memory is significantly dimmed in your imagination. What changes did you notice this time?

9. Finish this stage by bringing the brightness of your picture back to its original level.

10. Now, thinking back to your original experience and remembering how excited and enthusiastic you felt, step back into that experience, listening carefully to all the sounds around you, noticing how noisy it is, how fast people are speaking and the tones of voice they are using. How high or low is the pitch of the different voices? What directions are they coming from? Pay attention to the pattern of those sounds: do they have a particular rhythm? Can you hear all the sounds clearly? Notice whether or not you are listening to any internal dialogue chattering away in your head.

11. While you listen to those sounds, pay close attention to the physical feelings that you may be experiencing in your body. If you were to give a name to the emotions attached to those feelings, what would it be? As you are experiencing all of those feelings, pay attention to just how intense those feelings are.

12. As you are listening to all of those sounds, change the volume of those sounds using a volume control, similar to one on a radio, knowing that you can turn the volume back to normal at any time that you desire. Turn up the volume of those sounds

and conversations, making them seem louder in your head than they originally were, stopping at the point where the individual sounds are still definable.

13. Now, pay attention to your feelings and whether the feelings that go with those sounds have changed in any way. How have they changed now that the sounds, the voices and noises, are louder?

14. Next, turn down the volume of those sounds, again knowing that you can readjust the volume later. Continue to turn down the volume control until the sounds in your mind become so quiet that you can barely hear them.

15. Again, pay attention to your feelings as your experience of that memory is significantly quietened in the echoes of your mind. What changes did you notice this time?

16. Finally, finish by bringing the volume back to its original level.

Emotional states and sub-modalities

Our emotional states are linked to the way we are thinking about things. If we are thinking about a problem and we are 'stuck', it may be that we are thinking about it in a 'stuck' sort of way. The make-up of 'stuck' will vary from individual to individual. If we gather information about the way a person is thinking about a problem, we may be able to shift (influence) the person's thinking style and therefore facilitate that person in solving the problem by changing the way he or she is thinking.

Our thinking patterns follow our representation systems of sight, sound, feelings, smells and taste. These representation systems or modalities have sub-modalities, and it is these sub-modalities that can affect our feelings and therefore our emotional state. In addition, at times these emotional states can get hard-wired into our physiology, in particular our body posture. Changing our body posture, the representation system we are using to think, as well as where we are looking, can have a significant effect on our emotional state.

Sub-modalities are a powerful mechanism for changing perspectives and influencing and, as such, are a powerful mechanism for creativity and leadership.

Sub-modalities

VISUAL	Associated (in the picture, seeing through your own eyes) Disassociated (looking at yourself in the picture, looking through an observer's eyes) Black and white or colour Brightness Size Shape Location and distance relative to self Contrast Clarity – blurred or focused Slide Movement/speed – film/slide show/photos Depth 3D/flat Framed or no frame	
AUDITORY	Words or sounds Digital (discontinuous sound, eg words) or analogue (continuous sound) Location and distance relative to self Pitch Tone – soft or harsh Voice (whose?) Rhythm Timbre (fullness of sound) Internal External Direction Tempo – fast or slow Volume Duration	
KINAESTHETIC	Internal feelings External or tactile feelings Location and shape Weight – light or heavy Duration/frequency Size Pressure – hard or soft	Emotions Temperature Movement Intensity – sharp or dull Moisture Texture (rough or smooth) Rhythm
OLFACTORY	Pungency Intensity Location Aroma Specific smell	**GUSTATORY** Sweet Sour Salty Bitter Specific taste

Anchoring

Imagine how useful and powerful it would be if you could recall those times that you were performing creatively, at will, so that you knew you would always be energized and resourceful whenever you needed **to be**. **Being** energized and resourceful is a necessary prerequisite for creativity and innovation to flourish.

Anchoring is a term to describe that process. You already use anchors all of the time. A fire bell generates the response of heading for the exits. There are almost certainly pieces of music and smells that bring back memories – school dinners is often an anchor. Other anchors stimulate non-activity, like car alarms. Most people ignore them because they are always just going off.

An anchor is any stimulus that evokes a consistent response pattern from a person. It can be received through any of the five representation systems. For example, if I ask people to think of how they experienced Christmas as a small child, they will normally recall a feeling of high excitement associated with receiving presents, Father Christmas, a Christmas tree, carols etc. This is comparable to Pavlov's dog salivating at the sound of a bell.

Anchoring is used to shape behaviours and feelings towards desired states and away from undesired ones.

Types of anchor

Behavioural stimuli:	Symbols:	Universals:
Visual	Metaphors	Analogies
Auditory	Slogans	Common experiences
Kinaesthetic	Brands	
Olfactory		
Gustatory		
Voice tone		
A physical action		
Gestures		
Locations		
Key words		

Conditions for setting an anchor

▓ The uniqueness of the anchor.

▓ The timing of the anchor – at the peak of the emotional experience / feelings.

▓ The intensity of the experience.

▓ The purity of the experience (ie there are not other anchors creating competing experiences).

▓ The person must be associated with the experience.

▓ Anchors can be created in any representation system (visual, auditory, kinaesthetic, olfactory, gustatory).

In the context of leadership, anchors are important because your behaviour and everything you say or do (or don't do) become anchors for others. I often hear people telling me, 'We are asked to take risks and when you do you get beaten up.' The anchor is set and thereafter many people who start to think about something that equates to risk also equate it to getting beaten up and immediately stop thinking. Well done, you beater up of people, whoever you are!

'The beatings will continue until morale improves.'

Creating a state of personal excellence

1. Identify two experiences, one in which you were creative and your performance was highly effective and one in which you experienced difficulty and your performance was less than satisfactory. This could be related to a class of situations in which you would like more flexibility or a particular situation that you know is coming up.

2. Set up two separate locations for the two states on the floor, in order to keep the two states pure.

3. Stepping into the **desired state**, identify the physiology, the internal thinking patterns and sub-modalities as appropriate, asking questions such as:
   - What am I **seeing, hearing** and **feeling** both **externally** and **internally**?
   - Is there any internal dialogue going on?
   - What are the **sub-modalities** of those representation systems?
   - What am I doing that means this experience is so effective?

4. Moving out of the desired state location, break state using suggestions such as 'Imagine what it would feel like to have a lump of ice put down your back' or 'Imagine yourself doing cartwheels down Pall Mall.'

5. Now move into the **present state**, again identifying the physiology, the internal thinking patterns, the sub-modalities, asking questions such as:
   - What am I **seeing, hearing** and **feeling** both **externally** and **internally**?
   - Is there any internal dialogue going on?
   - What are the **sub-modalities** of those representation systems?
   - What am I doing that means this experience is so unsatisfactory?

6. Moving out of the **present state** location, break state using suggestions such as 'Imagine what it would feel like to have a

lump of ice put down your back' or 'Imagine yourself doing cartwheels down Pall Mall.'

7. Identify the differences between the two states.

8. Move back to the **desired state** and strengthen and anchor as follows:
   - Adjust any appropriate sub-modalities of the **desired state** to deepen the state. Do this by imagining a control knob. If you want more volume, turn up the control. If you want clearer images, adjust the contrast, etc.
   - Ask yourself if there is a word, symbol, metaphor, story, memory or feeling that is representative of this desired state and is easily recalled; make a contract with yourself to agree on this signal / anchor for the desired state when the feeling of the state is at its strongest.

9. Ascertain how to get from the **present state** to the **desired state**, noticing the positive intention of the present state. What lifeline can you throw to help you get there?

10. Walk from the **desired state** to the **present state**, noticing the transformation that occurs in the process. **Pay particular attention to how the feelings associated with the previous present state now become a resource for achieving the desired state.**

Creating an anchor and chaining emotional states using metaphor

You can create a similar experience by building the state in stages. I have used the following with a person who needed to step on to a conference platform in the morning and create a fully focused, energized model to get the day off to a great start. He finished the journey as a roaring tiger, a friendly one with pussycat tendencies, I hasten to add. He put the image on the mirror in his hotel room where he would see it the moment he woke up. It worked beautifully for him:

1. How are you feeling now – physically as well as emotionally?

2. How would you like to feel for the rest of the day and/or a particular occasion for which you would like to be in a 'good' physical and emotional state?

3. Set up four spots on the floor (in a line, one step apart) that will represent your current state, your desired state (for today and/or another occasion) and two intermediate states in between.

4. If you were to give an animal (or plant) name to your current state, what would it be?

5. If you were to give an animal name to your desired state, what would it be?

6. Move to the spot on the floor of your current state. Notice how this animal is feeling and move into the actual physical posture.

7. Move to the first transitional state. What animal might represent this state? How is this animal feeling, and how would this animal be standing?

8. Do the same for the next transitional state.

9. Moving into your desired state, notice this animal and how it is feeling; move into the actual physical posture.

10. Moving back to the beginning, walk through all four 'moods', keeping one foot in each state until the new state kicks in.

11. In the last spot, once the desired state is reached, imagine feeling like this during the rest of today and/or the other occasion and decide on the anchor or signal that will remind you of this state (action, gesture, symbol, word, picture, location, voice tone etc).

Using imaging to achieve goals and create new behaviours

Your mind uses the same neurological circuits either to remember actual experiences or to construct imaginary experiences. If you can use your imagination to create a vivid enough experience of achieving a goal or using a new behaviour, then you will find that you can do what you have imagined. This is what all the top performers do, especially sportsmen/women and salesmen/women.

Many people live their lives as if they are in a dress rehearsal, putting off their dreams and wishes for another day. Life is not a dress rehearsal – you can start using your mind to create the life you want. The exercises in subsequent sections will show you how to use imaging to create the results you want in your life.

'I never hit a shot even in practice without having a very sharp, in-focus picture of it in my head. It's like a colour movie. First I see the ball where I want it to finish, nice and white, sitting up high on the bright green grass. Then the scene quickly changes and I see the ball going there: its path, trajectory and shape, even its behaviour on landing. Then there's a sort of fade-out, and the next scene shows me making the kind of swing that will turn the previous images into reality.'

Jack Nicklaus, *Golfing My Way*

Use imaging to experience achieving your goals

1. Choose a goal and check that it satisfies the conditions for a well-formed outcome (see earlier section).

2. Imagine what it will be like when you have achieved your goal. Create an image of it in your mind's eye.

3. **Physically step** into the picture and actually experience what it is like to have achieved your goal. Make the experience more compelling by enhancing the relevant sub-modalities, eg make the images brighter, add colour and movement, add congratulatory sounds and voice tones, including inner dialogue. Walk around in the picture and notice different perspectives.

4. What are you seeing and hearing around you that lets you know you have succeeded and achieved the results you wanted? What are you saying to yourself internally, what are you doing and what does it feel like?

5. What are those around you seeing and hearing you doing? What are they saying about you/your goal? Step into their shoes and experience what they are feeling.

6. **Physically jump back out of the scene** and experience the steps it took to get you to your final outcome, repeating steps 3 to 5.
   - What are you seeing and hearing around you, what are you saying to yourself internally, what are you doing and what does it feel like?
   - What are those around you seeing and hearing you doing? What are they saying about you/your goal? Step into their shoes and experience what they are feeling.

7. Write down the steps you took in an action plan, detailing what you will do and when.

Finding resources using a timeline

1. Define a space on the floor as your timeline with the future in front of you and the past behind you.

2. Choose a point on the line as the present.

3. Identify a goal you wish to achieve or a time when you wish to be in a particularly resourceful state.

4. Step on to the line in your present state and notice what you are seeing, hearing and feeling, paying attention to the sub-modalities.

5. Walk into the future until you reach your desired state and again notice what you are seeing, hearing and feeling, paying attention to the sub-modalities.

6. Identify the resources that you most wish to have with you in the desired state and for each of them walk back down your timeline into your past, noticing the times you had each of these resources.

7. Focus on the resource at the earliest point on your line and let yourself build up into a state of being full of that resource. When you are fully resourceful, anchor the state using your preferred way and move up the line to the next point of the same resource. Let this state grow in you by seeing, hearing and feeling and then set the anchor again. Continue collecting the resource and finally walk this newly enhanced resource state up to the desired state in the future and set an anchor for this time.

8. Repeat the process for as many different elements of resource as you wish to gather.

Now, take some time to consider your experience of the previous exercises and notice what this suggests for encouraging creativity in yourself and creativity in others:

▓ How many of your current actions raise the probabilities for successful creative effort?

▓ How many are achieving the reverse?

▓ What are the anchors in your life and how are they influencing you and others?

▓ Are these the intended outcomes?

▓ Are they useful outcomes?

▓ What could you do instead?

▓ What could you encourage others to do instead?

Seeing things from different perspectives

> *Problems cannot be solved by thinking within the framework within which the problems were created.*
>
> Albert Einstein

Perceptual filters and flexibility

'Perceptual filter' is the label that is used to describe how we see the world. How we see the world is coloured by our past experiences. I sometimes think of life as a kaleidoscope with each of the filters that create the different patterns being a different perceptual filter. These experiences are hard-wired into our neurology or nervous system, creating what we call 'perceptual filters'. We each have our own personal model of the world, which will have blind spots caused by these perceptual filters. It often pays to look at a situation from a different point of view or wider perspective in order to obtain greater understanding of what is going on.

In this part of the 'not-a-book', you will be focusing on perception from a 'point of view' (notice the language) of **being**. Later, in the Synectics Creative Problem-Solving Process, you will consider perception from a point of view of **doing**. Considering life from different perspectives is clearly important for creativity and innovation.

The more perspectives or points of view we have looked at and experienced, the more choices we have. This enables us to have greater flexibility and a better chance of producing a win–win outcome for all those concerned. Exploring a problem or opportunity from a number of different perceptual positions enables us to move beyond our customary habits and perceptions, bringing wisdom to our interactions with others.

Perceptual positions

These are the stances from which we think about a set of circumstances or a particular situation. The basic perceptual positions in communication and relationships are:

▓ **'First position' or 'Self' – I**
Being in your own skin, looking at the world through your own eyes, having your own point of view based on your own beliefs, assumptions and past experiences.

▓ **'Second position' or 'Other' – You**
Being in the 'shoes' of the other person, looking at the world through his/her eyes, having his/her point of view based on his/her beliefs and assumptions and as if you had experienced his or her life.

▓ **'Third position' or 'Observer' – They**
Being a detached observer of the relationship between you and the other person – like a fly on the wall, detached from the feelings of those involved in the situation.

▓ **'Fourth position' or 'Thinking vision of the system' – We**
Being part of a larger system, taking on the perspective of the whole system – ie department, organization or larger community.

The benefits of exploring perceptual positions

▒ To uncover blind spots in our perspective or internal map of the world.

▒ To understand better the perspectives of others in order to create win–win outcomes.

▒ To develop greater flexibility in both our thinking patterns and our behaviour.

▒ To increase the number of our options and thereby increase our creativity and our chances of success.

Using perceptual positions to explore a challenging project

Identify a challenging situation or project in which you will play a leadership role, involving a particular person/people. Choose a situation about which you would like greater understanding of the thoughts and emotions of the person/people involved:

1. Set up spaces on the floor for the four perceptual positions.

2. Step in the space of first position, imagining that the other person is in front of you in the space of second position. What are you seeing and hearing, externally, from your perspective? Is anything going on internally (such as internal dialogue)? What are you feeling?

3. Now step in the space of second position, in the shoes of the other person, with that person's physiology (body posture), beliefs and assumptions and seeing through that person's eyes. What are you seeing, hearing and feeling from this perspective?

4. Now move into the space of third position, looking at the relationship as if it were a video of these two people. How are they relating and what behaviours are they exhibiting? From this

perspective, is there anything that the person in first position could do differently?

5. Finally, move into fourth position, widening the angle of the video lens, looking at the system as a whole. Who else is involved in the situation? What would be in the best interests of the whole system? From this wider perspective, is there anything that the person in first position could do differently to influence the system as a whole or interact more effectively with the other person/people?

6. As you explore the different perceptual positions, notice how your experience of the interaction changes from the different perspectives. What new awareness did you get about yourself, the other person or what would be in the best interests of the whole system?

Reframing: the transformation of meaning

Reframing is a way of describing a situation differently, thereby assigning a different meaning to that situation – hence the transformation of meaning.

> *Instead of pouring knowledge into people's heads, we need to help them grind a new set of eyeglasses so that we can see the world in a new way.*
>
> J S Brown

> *A very old Chinese Taoist story describes a farmer in a poor country village. He was considered very well to do, partly because he owned a horse, which he used for ploughing and for transportation. One day his horse ran away. All his neighbours exclaimed how terrible this was, but the farmer simply said 'Maybe.'*
>
> *A few days later the horse returned and brought two wild horses with it. The neighbours all rejoiced at his good fortune, but the farmer just said 'Maybe.'*
>
> *The next day the farmer's son tried to ride one of the wild horses; the horse threw him and broke his leg. The neighbours all offered their sympathy for his misfortune, but the farmer again said 'Maybe.'*

> *The next week conscription officers came to the village to take young men for the army. They rejected the farmer's son because of his broken leg. When the neighbours told him how lucky he was, the farmer replied 'Maybe'...*

The meaning that we give to any event depends on how we perceive it. Our perception is often coloured by our past experiences, which have given rise to our current beliefs and values. I wrote earlier of my experience with several of my clients who are very keen to put things in themes and clusters that bring about immediate order and sense, even if this is not representative of any known market. I was working with one of the major banks, helping them to explore ways of constructing new products. We had a number of consumers working in the same room with the bank team. Using the bank's normal segmentation, three of the consumers were a single type for the bank's purposes. What the bank team discovered was that in reality each of the consumers was unique in certain ways and the bank would fail to sell to any of them using the old framing of 'a consumer'.

When seeking to be creative and when operating as leaders, we can discover great insights and provide great motivation by taking the **most useful meaning** from any situation in order **to achieve our desired outcomes.**

Reframing is the transformation of the meaning of an event by changing the frame of reference, ie by looking at a different perspective or within a different 'frame' or context. So, in the story above, having two horses is perceived to be a good thing until it is seen in the context of the son's broken leg. A broken leg seems very unfortunate until the conscription officers arrive the next week. When we change the perspective or context, we change the meaning.

Albert Einstein offers a wonderful reframe of difficulties or problems in his quote, **'in the middle of difficulty lies opportunity'.** In addition, working with opportunities is much more rewarding and less stressful than working with problems.

Reframing is also the pivotal element in the creative process, for example by putting a commonplace event in a new frame that may at first seem absurd.

> *A friend of physicist Donald Glaser pointed to a glass of beer and jokingly said, 'Why don't you use that to catch your sub-atomic particles?' Glaser looked at the bubbles forming in the beer, and went back to his lab to invent the 'bubble chamber', similar to the Wilson Cloud chamber, for detecting the paths of particles in high-energy physics experiments.*

Reframing failure as feedback

> *There is no such thing as a failed experiment, only experiments with unexpected outcomes.*
>
> Buckminster Fuller

This is more fun if you get together with a group of friends, though you can do it on your own:

1. Each person to think of an event in the past that he or she had previously considered a 'failure'.

2. Person A to describe the 'failure' to B, C and D.

3. In turn B, C and D each to think and describe either:
   - another meaning to give to the situation; or
   - another context in which the meaning is transformed.

   The more absurd the reframe the better! Try using reframes that are illegal or would get you fired.

4. Person A to describe what insights he or she has gained (and to come up with his or her own reframe?).

5. Repeat for each person…

Reframing an inner voice and developing an internal mentor

1. Identify an inner voice that has criticized you in the past.
    Think of a past event where an inner voice criticized you or made comments such as:

    - That's a stupid idea.
    - You can't say or do that; it's silly.
    - You're / that's not very creative.

    Step back in time into the situation and listen carefully to how the voice is speaking: the sounds, the voice tone, tempo and rhythm in which it is saying the words.

2. Discover your inner voice's positive intention.
    Ask the voice:
    - What is your positive intention? Or
    - What is it that you want to achieve for me by criticizing me in this way?

    Listen to the response and keep asking the questions until you can completely agree with the positive intention that you hear. For example:
    - It wants you to succeed / do well.
    - It wants you to look good (as opposed to keeping you from looking stupid).
    - It wants you to come up with the best / most creative ideas you can think of.

    This may include how the inner voice is responding, ie what quality of voice tone it is using – do you believe that it means it? Keep going until you are sure that it means it.

3. Acknowledge and thank the inner voice.
    Acknowledge the positive intention, agree with it and thank the inner voice for having this positive intention for you.

4. Ask the inner voice to join in a search for alternatives.
    Ask the inner voice, 'If there were other ways of achieving this positive intention that are at least as good as, and perhaps

better than, what you have previously been doing, would you be prepared to try them out?'

Wait until you have a 'Yes' response.

5. Get help from your internal mentor in finding alternatives.

   Identify an internal mentor or creative part of you which has been responsible for encouraging you in the past. Another alternative is to think of someone who has either encouraged you in the past or who is a role model you respect. (If you can't think of someone, make someone up.)

   Ask this internal mentor to help you with generating lots and lots of alternative behaviours to achieve the **positive intention** of your inner voice.

6. Ask the inner voice to choose the three best alternatives.

   Ask your original inner voice to choose three of the best alternative behaviours that it likes and believes will work as well as, or better than, what it had been doing in the past.

7. Future planning

   Actively imagine in your mind carrying out each of these three alternative behaviours in turn, in the appropriate situation, to find out how well each works.

   If some don't work so well, know that you can ask your internal mentor to generate more choices (as in step 5).

   When you have three new choices that both your inner voice and your internal mentor like, ask your inner voice if it will be willing actually to use one or more of these choices in the appropriate situations.

Speaking another person's language

Thinking and learning styles

The language that a person uses will often reflect how he or she is thinking about something and / or the person's preferred learning style. Matching your language patterns to another person's thinking or learning style will enable you not only to improve your sphere of influence but to increase your ability to get your message across to others without distortion. Developing language patterns that cover a range of thinking and learning styles will enable you to communicate and motivate others more easily and also to create presentations that will appeal to a wider audience. Exploring the language patterns can become a creative process in itself – think of an author seeking many different ways to express emotion, create a picture using words etc.

Just as a computer runs 'application programs' that specify how that computer will manage any data input to the program, so people run programs. They are called **meta-programs**. The **typical** behaviour of an individual gives a clue to these **meta-programs**.

When people are thinking, they may be using any of their senses to experience or create that thinking process. Thinking styles can be ascertained by listening to the language that they use. This can be expressed in both individual words and the metaphors that a person uses. The following passage will allow you to identify your preferred representation system or thinking style.

Meta-program Patterns	
General Approach	▨ Move 'away' from problems or 'towards' goals. ▨ Be 'proactive' or 'reactive'.
Chunk Size	▨ Details – small chunks of specific information. ▨ Generalities – big picture.
Time Frames	▨ Focus on short, medium or long term. ▨ Focus on past, present or future.
Basic Cognitive or Thinking Style	▨ Vision – visualization. ▨ Action – movement. ▨ Logic – verbalization. ▨ Emotion – feelings.
Situational Emphasis	▨ Task – bias towards procedures or options. ▨ Relationship – bias towards self or others.
Analytical Style	▨ Similarities – matching. ▨ Differences – mismatching.

Which house would you prefer to live in?

The first house is a distinguished and visually attractive red-brick three-storey house set in its own grounds. The garden surrounds the house, so whichever aspect you view from the windows you can see flowers and trees. There is much natural light in the house. Decorations and colours can be chosen at your own discretion.

The second house harmonizes all you could wish for in a home. It is in a quiet position and whichever window you open you can hear birds singing and the trees gently swishing in the breeze. The construction of the house is such that if you were in one room talking to a neighbour and the children are shouting and playing loud music, you would not be able to hear each other. It is a house that is in tune with the different needs of people today.

The third house is extremely cosy. There is a sense of warmth and feeling at home. When people step over the threshold the first thing that grabs them is how comfortable and settled they feel. As you walk through the different rooms in the house you experience a feeling of satisfaction and pleasure.

They are the same house, as you will have worked out.

Verbal predicates and representation systems

Our senses are our doorways to perception; we each create our map of the world through our senses. There are five sensory modalities or representation systems. These are reflected in our language and the words and metaphors that we use.

Listening to a person's language gives you many clues about how that person is thinking and the nature of his or her internal representations and upon which senses they are based. These sensory-based words are known as 'predicates' and they can be words, phrases or metaphors.

The following list includes the predicates that are most widely used:

Visual	Auditory	Kinaesthetic	Olfactory	Gustatory
see	hear	feel	smell	taste

Further examples are shown on the following pages.

We all use all of the representation systems and we tend to have preferences. When communicating with someone it is useful to speak his or her language. You would not speak English to a French person and expect to be understood. Similarly, speak visually to a kinaesthetic person and you will sometimes find it hard to get your meaning across.

As a person who has to communicate to many, you will need to be able to communicate in as many representation systems as possible.

Internal pictures

Visual constructed V^c   **Visualization**   **Visual remembered V^r**

Internal sounds

Auditory constructed Λ^c   **Auditory remembered Λ^r**

Internal feelings   **Internal dialogue**

Kinaesthetic K   **Auditory digital A^d**

NB About 1 in 5 people have the reverse eye accessing cues – they are generally left-handed as well!

One way of identifying systems is clearly to listen; another is to watch eye movements. The following diagram is represented as though you are looking at the person. Always calibrate someone first. Ask the person to describe a situation and notice the language he or she uses and match this to eye accessing cues.

'Visual – seeing' words, phrases and metaphors

Appear	It *appears* that we have different points of *view*.
Blind	He has a *blind* spot.
Bright	Look on the *bright* side.
Clear	The ideas are *clear* to me now.
Dark	He was in a *dark* mood.
Dim	I take a *dim* view of that.
Eye	We do not see *eye to eye*.
Foresee	We failed to *foresee* the consequences.
Gleam	At last the light is *gleaming* from the end of the tunnel.
Heave	They *hove* into view.
Image	He's the *image* of his father.
Look	*Looking* at it from a different *perspective*.
Outlook	The *outlook* remains cloudy.
Perspective	Let's take a different *perspective* on the problem.
Picture	*Picture* the business in five years.
See	Try to *see* things from my point of *view*.
Transparent	His strategy is *transparent*.
View	What is your point of *view*?
Watch	*Watch* your step.
X-ray	He must have *X-ray* vision.
Yellow	They have a *yellow* streak.

'Auditory – hearing' words, phrases and metaphors

Bell	Clear as a *bell*.
Call	Who's *calling* the tune here?
Deaf	Turn a *deaf* ear.
Echo	I *echo* your words.
Gong	It was like a *gong* in my head.
Harmony	Living in *harmony*.
Knock	It came to me like a *knock* on the door.
Listen	Just *listen* to yourself.
Melody	The different parts of the business are like a *melody*.
Noise	The corporate *noise* is confusing the issue.
Patter	Too much management *patter* with no substance.
Quiet	We need *quiet* time to think.
Resonate	That *resonates* with me.
Shout	You're *shouting* from the rooftops.
Silence	Your *silence* speaks volumes.
Tone	The *tone* of the discussion.
Volume	The expression on his face spoke *volumes*.
Wavelength	They're on the same *wavelength*.
Yell	It was like a *yell* from hell.

'Kinaesthetic – feeling' words, phrases and metaphors

Ache	It affects me like an *ache* in my heart.
Balance	How can we maintain a sense of *balance*?
Cool	He's a *cool* customer.
Dig	It feels like someone is *digging* into my body.
Effort	The *effort* of making the changes feels too great.
Feel	I can *feel* it in my bones.
Grasp	I can't *grasp* your point.
Hot	Too *hot* to handle.
Insensitive	He's so *insensitive*.
Knife	He was through the company like a *knife* through butter.
Lull	We were *lulled* into a false sense of security.
Mutilate	The way he deals with people is a *mutilation* of normal values.
Pull	*Pull* yourself together.
Queasy	The plans leave me with a *queasy* feeling in my stomach.
Rub	*Rub* me up the wrong way.
Smooth	He's a *smooth* operator.
Tangible	We need *tangible* outcomes.
Uptight	He is a very *uptight* character.
Wet	What a *wet* blanket.

'Olfactory – smelling' words, phrases and metaphors

Aroma	The *aroma* is somewhat musty.
Bouquet	What a lovely *bouquet*.
Cheesy	The whole idea seems rather *cheesy*.
Dank	The room was like a *dank* dungeon.
Effluent	About as appealing as *effluent*.
Fresh	Like *fresh* air blowing through the building.
Incense	I could imagine the sweet smell of *incense*.
Odorous	He has an *odorous* personality.
Roses	Comes up smelling of *roses*.
Stinks	Your ideas *stink*.
Tainted	His ideas are *tainted* by gossip.
Whiff	I smelt the *whiff* of corruption.

'Gustatory – tasting' words, phrases and metaphors

Appetite	An *appetite* for the good life.
Bitter	It left a *bitter* taste in the mouth.
Chew	We'll *chew* the ideas over.
Flavour	There are many *flavours* of people.
Ginger	*Ginger* it up to make it more interesting.
Honey	His *honeyed* tones.
Insipid	He is an *insipid* character.
Juicy	I heard some *juicy* gossip.
Lemon	It had the piquancy of a *lemon*.
Orange	It was like sucking *orange* peel.
Spice	We have to *spice* our ideas up.
Taste	I can *taste* the success.

A comparison of predicates for different representation systems

Neutral	Visual	Auditory	Kinaesthetic
I don't agree	We don't see eye to eye	We are not on the same wavelength	Our ideas clash
Absent	Blank	Dumb, silence	Numb
Attentive	Keep your eyes peeled	Listen carefully	Take care of
Attitude	Perspective, viewpoint	Comment, opinion	Stance
Balance	Symmetry	Harmony	Tranquillity
Conceive	Imagine	Call up, recall	Get a hold of
Consider the idea	Look at the idea	Sound out the idea	Get a grip on the idea
Demonstrate, direct	Show, illuminate, illustrate	Explain, instruct, talk through	Sort out, lead through, lay out, walk through
Display	Show off	Sound off	Put on parade
Emit	Radiate, glow	Resonate, hum	Vibrate
Go over	Look over	Talk over	Walk through
Identify	Point out	Call attention to	Put the finger on
Ignore, miss	Overlook	Tune out	Pass over, let slide
Insensitive	Blind	Deaf	Unfeeling
Intensity	Brightness	Volume	Pressure, weight
Notice	Flash on, look around	Tune into, listen in	Get a hold of, get a feel for
Ostentatious	Showy, flashy, colourful	Loud	Striking
Perceive	See	Hear	Feel
Persevere	See it through to the end	Hear it out to the end	Stick with it, carry through with it
Plain	Lacklustre	Muted	Dull, sluggish
Refer to	Point to	Allude to	Touch upon
Reminds one of	Looks familiar	Rings a bell	Strikes one as familiar
Repeat	Review	Rehearse	Rerun
I understand what you mean	I see what you mean	I hear what you are saying	I feel I have got hold of it

Exploring representation systems and channels in presentations

1. Pick an idea or concept that is important, challenging to you or you want to be more creative about.

2. Design a presentation of the idea/concept or opportunity/ problem using words alone (auditory channel).

3. Develop other ways of presenting the same idea/concept, ie using different communication channels to appeal to different thinking styles/representation systems:
   - a picture or symbol;
   - a metaphor or analogy;
   - a demonstration;
   - different types of sensory-based language.

4. Notice how you have created a number of new perspectives and frames. You may choose to reflect upon just how many options you may have dismissed on some occasions in the past.

Rapport and influencing skills

Rapport is the process of building and maintaining a relationship based on mutual understanding and trust. It is a way of entering another person's map of the world in order to build understanding. It is an extension of what people do naturally and unconsciously.

In the context of creativity, innovation and leadership, this is a key process for being in other people's worlds, getting into their internal map. Someone who cannot get into rapport with a wide range of people will be a poor communicator. Collaborative working for group creative problem solving is a major skill for developing innovative businesses.

You will know from your own experiences of **being** as you have read through this book that, unless you make contact at the level of **being,** you are making only very superficial contact with people.

The impact of verbal/non-verbal communication

It is worth noting that voice, gestures and body posture play an important part in communication. Only 7 per cent of communication is in the words that people use (the result of research done in the 1970s by a psychologist, Albert Mehrabian).

The relative impact of the different communication channels is shown over the page.

Words or Content	Ideas Text	7%
Voice	Tone Quality Volume Clarity	**38%**
Physical or Non-Verbal	Body language Posture/physiology Eye movements Hand gestures Body movements	**55%**

'Actions speak louder than words'

In a presentation situation, in order to ensure that your message comes across congruently, it is important that your verbal and non-verbal messages are in agreement, ie back each other up. It's not what you say, but how you say it that will have the greatest impact.

Summarized below are some of the key elements of rapport. You may find you do many of these naturally, and for others you will have to spend time noticing how your performance in that aspect coincides with others, and how it does not.

Breathing, for example, is an important aspect of rapport and, because it is so natural to us, we rarely focus on it. Next time someone comes to you and is 'breathless with excitement', try matching that person's rate of breathing for a while and see how this changes the way you experience being with him or her. (Warning, if the person is hyperventilating, do not try to match the breathing until the person has calmed down a bit.)

Non-verbal skills

Matching:

Voice quality	■	Tone, tempo, volume.
Physiology/posture	■	Whole body matching.
	■	Half body matching.
	■	Angle of head and shoulders.
Breathing	■	Breathing in time with the other person.
Gestures	■	Facial expressions.
	■	Hand gestures.

Cross-over matching:

Matching one aspect of your behaviour to a different aspect of the other's behaviour	■	Tapping your pencil in time to the other's footsteps.
	■	Pacing eye blinks with head nods or finger movements.

Other aspects of rapport:

Active listening	■	Placing your entire attention on the other person, listening attentively, encouraging him or her with non-verbal communication, eg smiling, nodding.

Verbal skills

Matching:

Predicates	▨ Visual.
	▨ Auditory.
	▨ Kinaesthetic.
	▨ Olfactory.
	▨ Gustatory.
Backtracking	▨ Going back over what was said and done (in sequence) to ensure that you have the correct understanding.
Paraphrasing	▨ Summarizing your understanding using the other's key words and phrases.

Logical levels:

Match the level that the other is talking about	▨ Vision/spirit.
	▨ Identity.
	▨ Beliefs and values.
	▨ Capabilities.
	▨ Behaviours.
	▨ Environment.

Matching and mismatching; pacing and leading

Building rapport is a key skill in any situation where you wish to build trust and increase your influence. It is also an important skill when creating the supportive group climates that allow creativity and innovation to flourish.

The sequence to building rapport and influencing others

▓ **Match** the other person's behaviour.

▓ **Pace** the other person's behaviour by continuing to match his or her behaviour.

▓ Start to **lead** the other person by incrementally changing an aspect of your behaviour in order to shift the other person's pattern of behaviour to something else.

▓ If the other person rejects your lead, then go back to pacing him or her.

▓ If he or she accepts your lead, then continue to lead.

It is worth noting that mismatching can, on occasion, be as important as matching, eg changing one's voice tone and speed in order to bring a telephone conversation to a close.

Matching is not mimicry. As you begin to experiment with rapport skills, it will seem strange at first because you are focusing on behaviour that is usually in your subconscious. Later, it will revert to a more natural feel. Be aware of getting into mimicry in your early attempts.

If you are noticing doubts in your mind about the power of rapport skills, imagine talking English to a non-English-speaking Chinese. Rapport will be easier if you both speak one another's language. Language is more than words – breathing is a language and gestures are a language. (By the way, you can be in rapport with someone whose language you do not speak; you just will not be able to communicate as easily or effectively).

Try this as a game. Get a group together, maybe four of you, and deliberately match and mismatch one another using the different elements of rapport. Talk about holidays, sport or business and notice how different the experience is.

Levels of leadership and leadership style

Now is the time to begin to pull together your experiences of **being** and consider these in the context of leadership and leadership style designed to encourage and support creativity and innovation in the organization. Leadership may refer to how you provide leadership for others or it may refer to how you choose to lead your own life.

You may have noticed, as you have considered the aspects of **being** that I have introduced, just how many styles are available and, as I wrote towards the very beginning of this book, the more flexibility you have available to you the more contexts in which you can operate effectively.

As part of a major study of leadership skills at Fiat, Robert Dilts applied logical levels to the leadership styles identified by Bass in 1985, which included both transactional and transformational categories of leadership. These leadership styles, especially at the transformational levels, are more about state and less about actions and, therefore, are useful communication and influencing styles for a variety of situations. Different styles or a mixture of several of them may be appropriate, depending on the context or situation. The styles associated with the different levels of change are shown in the following table.

	Leadership style	Influence is directed towards the following level of change:
Transformational	**Charismatic/'Idealised influence'** Give a sense of purpose or mission.	**Identity** Managing the Who?
	Inspirational Motivate to do one's best. **Individualized consideration** Express concern for individual's feelings and values.	**Beliefs** Managing the Why? and **Values** Managing What's important?
	Management by objective Provide clear goals and targets. Intellectual stimulation. Draw out critical thinking abilities.	**Capabilities** Managing the How?
Transactional	**Contingent reward** Define clear preferences and consequences of actions.	**Behaviour** Managing the What?
	Management by exception Make no corrective actions unless there is a problem.	**Environment** Managing the Where? and When?

Walking into the future, integrating your leadership style(s)

Earlier in the book, when I first wrote about **being**, I introduced logical levels and you experimented with these. I said you would revisit them, and now is the time, knowing that you know so much more about yourself and the internal maps that you use to create your realities in the external world.

Aligning logical levels

1. Choose a goal, project or presentation in which you will be participating or for which you will be playing a leadership role and where you want to be as resourceful and creative as possible.

2. Physically lay out a space for each of the six logical levels: Spiritual/Vision, Identity, Beliefs and Values, Capabilities, Behaviours, Environment. In sequence, move into each of the six spaces, answering the questions shown below.

3. **Environment**: 'When and where will you be participating in or leading this project or achieving this goal?'

4. **Behaviours**: 'What will you be doing in those times and places? What actions will you be taking?'

5. **Capabilities/Skills**: 'How will you be carrying out those actions and behaviours? How will you be using your mind? What capabilities/skills do you have or need in order to do those actions in those times and places?'

6. **Beliefs and Values**: 'Why do you want to use those skills to accomplish those activities? What values are important to you when you are involved in those activities? What's important about those activities?'

7. **Identity**: 'Who are you if you have those beliefs and values and use those capabilities to accomplish those behaviours in that

environment? What role are you playing? What is a metaphor or symbol for your Identity and Mission?'

8. **Spiritual/Vision**: 'Who and what else is involved? What is the vision beyond yourself that you are participating in? What is a metaphor or symbol for your vision?'

9. Taking that experience (including body posture and feelings) of your Vision with you, move back into the **Identity** space and notice how it enriches your initial experience of your Identity and Mission.

10. Take your experience of both your Vision and your Identity back to the **Beliefs and Values** space and notice how they enrich and enhance your initial experience of your Beliefs and Values.

11. Take all those experiences of your Vision, Identity, Beliefs and Values back into the **Capabilities** space. Notice how they strengthen, change and enrich your experience of your Capabilities and Skills.

12. Take all of the previous levels into the **Behaviour** space. Notice how your Behaviours are reflections and manifestations of all the higher levels within you.

13. Bring all levels of yourself into the **Environment** space and experience how it is transformed and enriched.

14. Notice what this aligned state feels like and imagine how it will be when you are experiencing this state at key times and places in the future when you will most need it.

Aligning your verbal and non-verbal/behavioural messages or 'how to walk your talk'

1. Decide on a message that you want to get across in either a presentation or another type of meeting.

2. Determine the logical level(s) you wish to influence and the leadership style you wish to use.

Environment	Where and when?	Management by exception
Behaviours	What?	Contingent reward
Capabilities and Skills	How?	Management by objective Intellectual stimulation
Beliefs and Values	Why? What's important?	Inspirational Individualized consideration
Mission and Purpose	Who?	Charismatic/Idealized influence

3. In addition, define any non-verbal messages you would like to communicate in relation to your verbal message, including:
   - your emotional state (eg confident, excited);
   - how you want to interact with your audience – the type of relationship you want to have with your audience (ie boss or collaborator, manager or coach/facilitator);
   - the desired emotional state for your audience to be in (eg open-minded, alert, relaxed).

4. Determine how you want to use voice tones, gestures, body posture, room set-up/spatial location etc to communicate the relevant non-verbal message.

Now that you have experienced **being**, one of your key tasks is to use this knowledge to live your life to the full and, as a leader, to help others do the same. This is the journey described right at the beginning of this book, and represented as the **Human Being** stream in **Enterprise Innovation**.

You may think it will take for ever for many people to experience the journey. The more the leaders in a business experience this journey **and live the results**, the clearer model they demonstrate to the people in the business and the easier **and faster** the journey will be. Think about it: if you set off on a car journey with a clear road map, it is easier to navigate and you do not get lost; so it is with people.

You are the leader; you are the map.

This part of the book is about

Doing

Some things to *do* so that you can *do*

This section of the book introduces tools and techniques for creativity and innovation that you may find useful in the **Human Doing stream**. Businesses work by people **doing** things. Typically, activity involves groups of different sizes. Most activities are time-bound with a beginning and an end, which is the classic definition of a project.

The **Human Doing stream** is about running creative problem-solving meetings and effective meetings generally in order to get to outcomes for the business. The tools include ways of managing the climate, ways to get ideas and ways to turn these ideas into action.

The tools that are described, and the structures for using them given in Appendix 1, are the core elements of Synectics. They are a distillation of behaviours based upon observation of successful creativity and innovation sessions, where open-mindedness, flexibility, and clear and open communication are very important.

Life, particularly business life, is a series of problem-solving meetings. Often, you may not think of them in that framing but, as a process, most meetings contain elements of problem solving. Considering another perspective, being open to other views and feelings, making choices and turning the choices into decisions and actions are what people **do**, ie problem solving.

Putting the people together

and learning about

one another

Building star teams

From your exploration of **being**, you now have a real insight into just how diverse people are. It follows that in order to have groups of people working together effectively they need to **be** together. This means **being** together mentally and, from time to time, physically.

In my own company, we work as **'virtual teams'**. We operate a process we call **'entrepreneurial teamwork'**. It is designed to ensure that anyone who joins us has the capability to survive alone, because experience has shown us that this capability is necessary to survive when doing our type of work. We are also very clear that it is necessary to have support from time to time, and we need to operate in groups in order to work on larger projects and to generate high-quality solutions for our clients.

Meeting as a team has become more important to us since we decided running a large office as an overhead was pointless.

The concepts and set of tools described in the following pages are all designed to help you generate supportive climates for working together, because supportive climates are more productive, as described in an earlier chapter.

My own experience is that I can take a typical company meeting and, by working with the participants to restructure the agenda and modify behaviour, reduce the time it takes by half, double the amount of work done and raise the level of creativity. Have you ever counted how much money people spend in your business sitting in meetings? If you want to save costs, start by looking at how you manage meetings.

I know of one company that ran a Tuesday meeting for 10 plant management staff. The plant manager decided to focus on what was taking place at the meetings. He noticed that many decisions already made were brought to the meeting so that if they went wrong a manager could point out that everyone had agreed with the decision in the meeting. He insisted decisions were made at the point where accountability lay. Eventually the agenda emptied out so much they stopped having the meeting. Imagine the cost of having 10 senior managers in a meeting for a day!

When you begin to think about putting groups together, start with the roles.

Finding a way to achieve action-oriented meetings

A London manufacturing plant for a drinks-producing company turned to Synectics to revamp completely the way their weekly meetings were run. The management team was spending up to four hours every Tuesday morning in a 'control meeting', designed to allow the group to review and make decisions on important plant operational issues. The meeting was regarded as a trial to attend, always overran its time allotment and many items were never discussed. Behaviour was a mix of aggression, politics, defence and constructive discussion. The balance was felt to be all wrong.

The challenge was to focus the meeting on constructive behaviour only, in order to shorten meeting times, improve the working environment, get more creative and get decisions made. At that time, Synectics innovative teamwork and project management programmes were already being used across the plant to change the way cross-functional teams worked together. This included introducing the 'agenda' meeting, a format for management and project reviews.

Once the management team introduced Synectics' agenda meeting structure into their 'control meeting', they achieved the following results:

1. Meetings are one hour long, never longer.

2. Minutes are recorded as bullet points at the time and e-mailed to all managers at the end of the meeting.

3. Every item has an owner, or it does not get on to the agenda.

4. An owner is expected to have dealt with any major barriers before the meeting, rather than collecting support outside and then using the meeting to gang up on the minority view.

5. Guidelines for behaviour encourage an open culture and positive feedback.

A consequence of this process is that many decisions are now taken outside the meeting, because managers realize that previously they were merely using meeting time to get commitment to decisions that were really the responsibility of the individual, not the group.

'It is a meeting that people do not want to miss. It has made us think about how we use our time, and has brought the issue of time and choice into people's minds. Frustration and anger in meetings have been enormously reduced.' Plant Director

The death of the chairperson

This is a popular concept in many businesses and may get you into trouble. The idea behind the metaphor will give you an opportunity to build supportive and cooperative meeting climates, essential for creativity and innovation to flourish.

The chair is often the most senior person in the room, ultimately the decision-maker, even if others apparently get a chance to make the right decision first before being overruled. The chair chooses who speaks, decides on agendas, directs the contents of the minutes and acts as the parent as necessary.

Not so far from the truth in many cases, this is also a description of two quite different roles, both of which one person can do to a degree, and neither is done as well as when you can focus on one at a time.

One role is concerned with **content**, the task that is being worked on. The second role is focused on the **processes of how people are working together**.

This is somewhat analogous to a football referee. He never kicks the ball; this is for the players. Left to their own devices they would get in each other's way, even given a set of rules to play to.

Pause here and consider how simple the game of football is, compared to a business meeting, especially one where new ideas and decisions are being discussed.

Why·is it then that we only consider playing football once we have a set of 'rules' **and a referee**? Yet people will calmly venture into all manner of highly complex business meetings with no thought to **how they are going to work together and who is going to control it all**.

In the early days of our research, we noticed how quickly people in groups get in each other's way, not always intentionally. It became clear that establishing the three roles described below dramatically improves the productivity of the group.

The role of the chairperson is in effect eliminated and split to become two roles, **facilitator** and **problem owner**. (I know not everything is a problem; maybe it is just a task. I also know problems can be **reframed** as tasks or opportunities. For the sake of convenience, I will use the role title **problem owner** in this section.)

Roles and responsibility

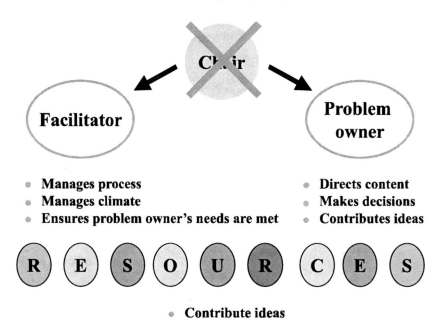

● **Contribute ideas**

Facilitator

▨ Concerned with process only, never involved in content.

▨ Sets positive climate by:
  – accepting all ideas;
  – writing down headlines of ideas, and solutions;
  – giving everyone a chance to contribute.

▓ Elicits the ideas hidden behind questions.

▓ Manages the time and pace of the meeting.

▓ Ensures the problem owner's best current thinking is shared with the group.

▓ Ensures that everybody takes notes of what is in his or her mind.

Problem owner

▓ Owns the issue.

▓ Describes it.

▓ Directs the content of the meeting by:
  - contributing wishes and ideas, selecting the avenues to explore, paraphrasing ideas to check understanding before evaluating;
  - evaluating constructively;
  - deciding when a solution has been reached;
  - committing to next action.

▓ Is accountable for results arising from decisions and actions.

The third role is that of **resource**.

Resource

▓ Generates ideas.

▓ Makes suggestions.

▓ Generates solutions.

▓ Gives opinions only when they are asked for.

Next time you get together in a meeting, ask everyone to state his or her role. If more than two people think they are the problem owner, you need to get this clear first. My instant test is to see who will get fired if the problem is not resolved. This is the problem owner. If that person is not in the room, your probability of implementing a solution has just gone down.

Sometimes I am told that 'We make decisions together.' In my experience, it is very rare for more than one person to be **accountable** for a decision. If you hear yourself saying this, take a good look and see if it is really true.

Metaphors *to be* together and grow understanding

A simple process for getting a group together and building deeper understanding of one another is to run a metaphor workshop:

■ Everyone in the group privately identifies a metaphor for themselves, one about what they do well, another about how they would like to be different or what they feel they should work on.

■ Identify two metaphors for every other person in the group – again, what you value about that person and how you would like him or her to be different.

■ Begin a round robin where you meet in pairs and share your metaphors with one another. Talk about yourself first and then your colleague.

■ At the end, share the picture of yourself in so far as you are comfortable to do so. You choose what to keep private.

The effect is that every person builds up a picture of himself or herself, based upon the metaphors. By using metaphors, you are having conversations that reach the **deep structure** rather than the more **surface structure** level of conversation that is more likely without metaphors.

We have done this ourselves from time to time and I treasure a metaphor about myself. A colleague described me as 'a great big American car, covered in shiny chrome, driving straight through the reception windows and announcing its arrival'.

He was telling me that he admired my drive and energy to make things happen (**doing**), and that my lack of sensitivity could sometimes get me into trouble (not so good at **being**).

This kind of meeting tends to be a lot of fun, and you learn a lot. It is in itself a creative experience as well, so you are beginning to tap into other **skills** and **capabilities** that are useful.

Questioning – the wisdom?

Getting the right balance between information and creativity

Think about the last time somebody invited you to help by giving some ideas. **Did you give an idea or did you ask a question?**

If a group of people gather in a room in order to do some creative problem solving, and the problem owner describes the problem, almost without exception the participants will begin to ask questions **in order to get more information so that they fully understand the problem.**

This wish for more information is positively meant. The group wants to be able to help the problem owner; therefore they wish to understand the problem.

Think about how you feel when operating in a fog of misunderstanding. Not very comfortable because you may get it wrong?

The problem owner can be pictured as a person in a hole in the ground, who is surrounded with so much information that he or she is unable to see any new directions in which to move.

A group, unencumbered with all this information, has the possibility of offering new perspectives.

They can pass down a ladder to new thoughts and possibilities.

Getting the right balance between information and creativity

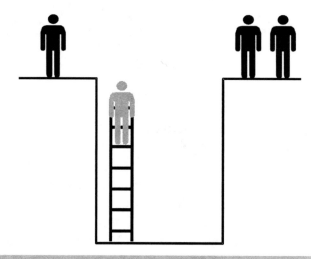

Brief task definition, avoid questions and respond with ideas

The alternative is that the group asks lots of questions until its members know as much as the problem owner, about the problem, and you are all in the hole together.

This can be very comforting for the problem owner, but you, the resource, have lost much of your ability to help.

Getting the right balance between information and creativity

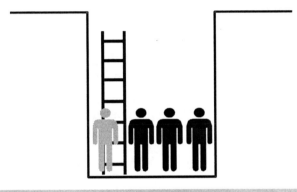

Long task definition, ask questions, collect information

You do not need as much information as you thought in order to give ideas.

Stay naïve!!

Children often have the interesting ideas because they do not know. **They guess.** Do some guessing and you will generate unusual perspectives. If you are truly looking to innovate, you cannot know the answer before you arrive – so who can say what is right or wrong?

In an innovation meeting, do not ask questions during the early stages of the problem definition and idea generation.

This comes as a surprise to you, perhaps? Try it and enjoy it!

In a previous chapter, the role of 'resource' was identified. Naïve resources, that is naïve about the task, can become a very important element in a creative problem-solving group. Experts get in the way in the early stages because they think they know – that is what expertise is about. Clearly, if the task needs problem solving, they do not know.

Naïve experts open up new perspectives. Within your organization, this widens the audience that can be invited to participate in helping the business solve problems. You can mix technical, finance, HR, admin, marketing etc, because as a naïve resource you do not need knowledge.

I once ran a session exploring research opportunities to improve replacement hips and knees. Aside from some surgeons, patients and the research group, we also invited architects, structural engineers, mechanical engineers, aeronautical engineers and micro-machine experts. They knew nothing of hips and knees and introduced wonderful new perspectives because of it. Questions were banned! Just guess and have an idea based upon that.

I want to focus your attention on two aspects:

the destructive nature of questions

and

hiding ideas behind questions

how they affect the climate of the meeting

Think for a moment

about the number of reasons you ask questions

and

why questions are asked of you.

List them here.

The destructive nature of questions

You may have drawn up a long list. Some of the reasons are 'legitimate' in the sense that they are questions asked for a genuine wish for the answer. Others lack this 'legitimacy', in that they are designed to demonstrate your personal superiority or someone else's stupidity.

I am not suggesting you use all of these reasons yourself; you will know the ones you use and why. However, it is clear that questions are used for many purposes.

You may have had the experience where someone has asked a question, the answer is given and the response from the questioner is:

'No, no! That's not what I meant at all...'

The respondent apparently got it wrong – and is feeling stupid and defensive because of this. He or she has been discounted!

Actually, what has happened is that the respondent guessed the wrong question from that long list of reasons why questions are asked. He or she gave the right answer to the wrong question, and is made to feel bad because of it.

Feeling bad is an inappropriate place to be in a climate that is designed to nurture trust and innovation. If you are going to ask a question in your meetings, say what is behind the question and take away the need for guessing.

Hiding ideas behind questions

A colleague of mine was running an innovation session where the problem concerned a scum that formed on top of a brew. This fell into the brew and destroyed the flavour.

The following question was asked:

'What temperature does the vat operate at?'

The answer was given as so many degrees by the problem owner, and the session continued.

During a break, the questioner was overheard talking to a colleague. He was saying what a pity it was about the vat temperature because, given an increase of x degrees, there is a chemical that would form the scum into a biscuit that could be lifted off.

The problem owner became excited, saying that the vat temperature was not that critical and could be changed so that the chemical could be used.

The idea was there all the time, and did not get into the innovation session because the resource asked a question instead of giving an idea.

How many ideas exist in you, and your organization, that are hidden because questions are asked instead of ideas being given?

How lazy we are with language

One of the major tools we have for communication is language. I imagine that most of you reading this book reckon you are pretty good at language. After all, you probably manage to get yourself understood most of the time.

However competent you are in your use of language, I am guessing you can make massive strides in the precision with which you speak.

The following is an overview of some of our most common language patterns. It includes the type of questions you may find helpful in order to get precision from **deletion**, **distortion** and **generalization**. You will recall these are the filters we use to programme from the external world into our internal maps.

Statement:	I am confused.
Question:	About what specifically?
	Where are you confused?
	When are you confused?
Statement:	I want to communicate better.
Question:	Better than what?
	What would be good enough?
Statement:	People just don't learn / listen.
Question:	What people specifically?
	Who specifically?
Statement:	I have difficulty in communicating.
Question:	How specifically are you communicating?
	What are you communicating specifically?

Statement:	I broke off the relationship.
Question:	How were you relating?
Statement:	Men should show emotions.
	People should take risks.
	People should be more creative.
Question:	What happens if they don't/aren't?
Statement:	I can't learn this material.
	We can't get senior managers out of the office for two days.
Question:	What stops you?
Statement:	If they knew the danger they would not take the risk.
Question:	How is it dangerous?
Statement:	The senior managers never listen to what we say.
Question:	Never? Has there never been a time when they listen?
Statement:	That film gives me the creeps.
Question:	How does it do that?
Statement:	That project worries me.
Question:	How does it worry you?
Statement:	They don't like being here.
Question:	How do you know they do not like being here?
Statement:	He's cool – he always wears purple.
Question:	How does wearing purple mean he's cool?
Statement:	It's wrong to interrupt.
Question:	Wrong according to whom?

You may have noticed some of these patterns are familiar to you. Possibly you will recall some memories from childhood, the way they were used on you by parents. If you are a parent, how many are you using now on your children? How often have you made remarks that are sweeping generalizations and could have been more meaningful?

I wonder how many times I have written similar sweeping generalizations in this book and will be hoisted by my own petard? (I have a wry grin on my face as I write this.)

A WORD OF WARNING!

This set of language patterns has a name. It is called the **meta model** or **precision model**. It has given rise to a new term, **meta murder**.

When using questions in order to elicit greater specificity, remember the **rapport** processes in the **being** section. It is possible to come across like a member of the Gestapo, and you will lose rapport with people, and most of your friends as well, if you try this at home.

Also notice the question **'Why?'** is not a part of this model.

Why?

This is usually the least useful question to ask in most contexts. It demands justification, and often information is more useful and results in greater understanding. It is particularly useless as a single word.

> **Why is it not possible to get products to market?**
> More useful will be
> **What is stopping you/the company getting products to market?**
> or make a statement
> **Give me three specific barriers to us getting products to market and an example of each.**

Discounting and revenge cycles: how to assume positive intent

Discounting is the process of putting people or their ideas down. Revenge cycles are what you get into when you get them back and criticize their ideas in turn.

Think about an occasion when you were in a meeting and somebody criticized somebody else's opinion or idea. The person who was criticized went quiet, and next contributed to the meeting when he or she spotted an opportunity to get back at the first person.

This often then develops into a game of tennis, each attempting to score points over the other. In most large corporations, there will be

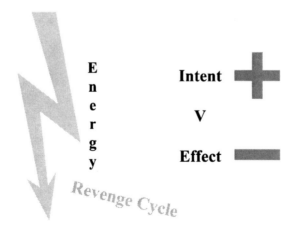

at least one pair, frequently among senior management, who go to a meeting in order to play revenge cycles, never to get any work done. Often this **discounting** of another person's opinions and ideas is unintentional. Given that this is the case, it is difficult for discounters to change their behaviour because they do not recognize that they are generating effects that they do not intend.

As the person feeling offended after being discounted, you can **choose to let the effect on you be positive rather than negative** and get into a cooperation cycle.

The intent–effect gap

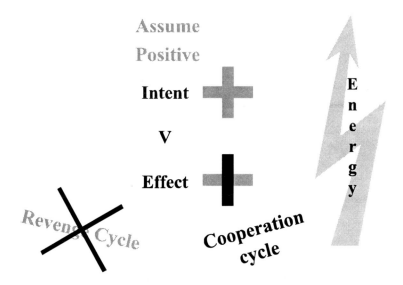

Next time someone criticizes your opinion, try this technique. Respond with something like:

> **'That is a very different view from mine. I would be interested to explore where we are agreeing and where we differ...'**

You will need to find a form of words that is natural to you. The difference in the interaction that follows will be quite dramatically different from your normal experience.

It may need the faith and commitment of a saint to do this and it will not be easy. You also have to mean it. If you are cynical about it, it will not work.

George Prince, one of the founders of Synectics, considers **assuming positive intent** as the single most powerful dynamic that can be introduced to meetings in order to build the supportive climate for openness, creativity and innovation.

Play the discounting game

Get into a pair or group of three with any friends or colleagues. One of you begins to wax lyrical to the other(s) about something you have heard, seen or experienced recently that you thought really terrific. The other(s) should discount the speaker in as many ways as possible.

Discounts are in three categories:

▨ **Oral** – 'That's rubbish!'

▨ **Tonal** – 'Really?' (said in an obviously cynical tone).

▨ **Non-verbal** – falling asleep.

You will be really good at this. Many of us discount a lot, often without realizing we are doing it. Talk about the effect this is having on one another.

A MESSAGE FOR EVERYONE WHO CHOOSES TO DISCOUNT DELIBERATELY, PLAYING CORPORATE POLITICS

We are all sensitive and that is how we are meant to be. If you are habitually poker-faced and overly assertive at work, think about how you are when with your family or friends.

Which is most natural to you? Which is most fun? Which will be most helpful in a meeting?

Listening: for ideas and to the meeting in your head

When you were at school, how often did you spend time in your own little world, staring into space or out of the window? Perhaps you rejoined the class when the board rubber made contact with your head, or the teacher screamed **'Pay attention!'** at you.

Now that you attend business meetings, how often do you suddenly come to with a start and recognize that your attention has wandered? Possibly your efforts to pay attention mean that when your chance to speak arrives you have forgotten what you wanted to say, or you will interrupt to avoid forgetting.

This describes experiences common to all of us. While someone speaks, or while you are reading this page, your mind will constantly be stimulated into thought of its own.

The thoughts you have will sometimes be clearly connected to the subject, or maybe they will have no obvious connection and you will be thinking, **'What made me think that?'**

Once your mind has been stimulated, you will tend to give your attention to this 'meeting' in your head, which is often more interesting than the public one in the room. You will **'drop out'**.

Your attention wanders (or wonders), and then you get hit on the head with the board rubber.

The following pattern of listening emerges.

Pattern of listening

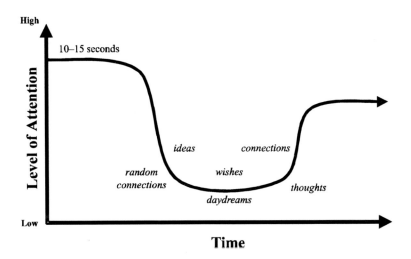

Your mind is a vast store of experiences and data. If I asked you to tell me everything you know, you are unlikely to be able to do this. Much of your personal database is in your subconscious mind.

The thoughts that you have when you are 'out' of the public meeting are a major source of ideas.

A typical speaking rate is 150–200 words a minute, yet your mind processes words at closer to 800–1,000 per minute. Therefore, your mind has the capacity to produce many thoughts, many ideas, while someone is speaking.

You were taught at school to listen so you could understand, to pay attention. This is appropriate in some circumstances.

You had a natural aptitude to listen to the meeting in your head and let your mind wander, which has now been disciplined out of you. This is the skill to relearn.

Remember how to be a child.

If you are invited to have ideas, it is not necessary to pay attention – better to let your mind wander so that it can tell you about the ideas it has.

Pattern of listening

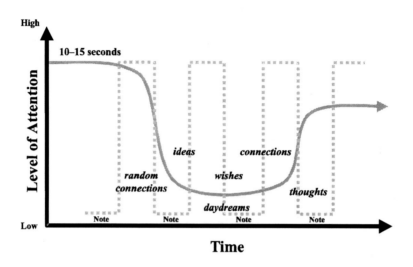

A technique called **in–out listening** will help you manage the meeting in your head so that you can use your mind for ideas.

Divide your notepad page into two columns.

On the left make lecture notes.

On the right make notes about thoughts, associations, connections, images, etc. Draw pictures if you wish.

When you are listening to the public meeting, make lecture notes.

When your attention level falls and you are listening to your head, make notes in the right-hand column.

The trick to learn is to avoid censorship and record your first thought, whatever it is. Often these thoughts may be ridiculous, impossible, rude, illegal or immoral. Try to avoid 'improving' them; gather the first thought.

It is yours and you do not have to share it; that will be your choice.

You will also find that this technique overcomes any tendency you may have to forget what it was you wanted to say, and it avoids the need to interrupt other people.

him/her:
lecture-type notes of
what the speaker is saying

me:
notes of my own
connections, images,
associations, thoughts
and ideas

Speaking for easy listening – giving ideas or opinions

Many of us are accustomed to giving our opinions and ideas in an environment where, frequently, every word is greeted with criticism. Unfortunately, such an environment is the norm for many business meetings.

Think for a moment about some of your recent experiences. Were you interrupted with a comment before you had time to finish what you were saying? How often is the response to your words something like: 'Yes, very interesting but…' or 'I hear what you say but…'?

So often, the response to your words is some level of attack, and you naturally defend yourself from this. A pattern for expressing ideas or opinions frequently looks like this:

Preamble

Sell

Main point

You may begin with a preamble, preparing the ground for the idea and checking out that the reception it is going to get is favourable. You then slip in the idea or opinion and quickly, before it can be criticized, sell it.

The 'sell' is designed to ensure everyone is absolutely clear about what a good idea you have expressed.

This process for speaking is time-consuming because of the high potential for 'waffle'.

Additionally, the idea may be lost because your audience has given up listening to you. Remember the in–out listening described earlier, and you will see how many of your audience may be listening to the meeting in their head rather than to you.

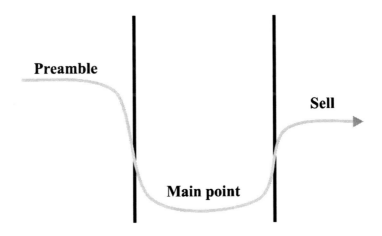

Now you know why the level of misunderstanding is so high in many meetings. Frequently, nobody heard what you actually said, only a version that was sort of related.

Headline and background is an alternative approach that will help you overcome the problem highlighted above.

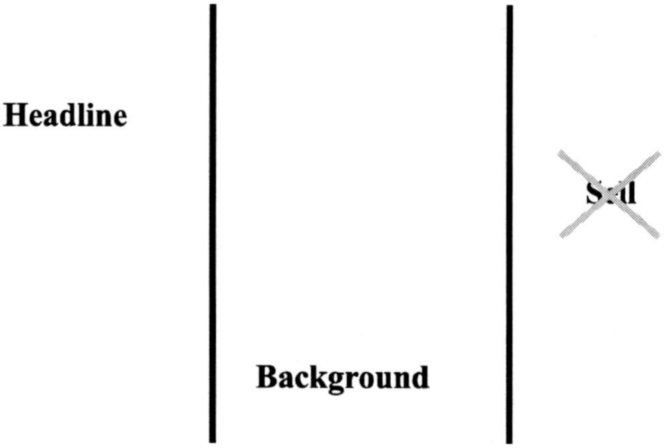

Headline

Sell

Background

Preface your ideas and opinions with a headline that positions the thought in the mind of the audience, like a newspaper headline. Follow the headline with some words of background that fill in a little of what you are thinking. There is no need to sell your viewpoint because this adds nothing to it. If your colleagues are using **in–out listening**, they can use the background as a trigger to further thoughts.

Problem-solving model

The following pages describe the elements of a
nine-step creative problem-solving model. This is
one of the four meeting structures described in
Appendix 1.

You will discover that problem-solving is what most of
your time is spent on, although you may not currently think
of it as that.

Nine-Step Synectics Problem-Solving Process

1. **Task Headline** from problem owner starting 'How to...'

2. **Task Analysis** from problem owner stating:
   - Why problem/opportunity
   - Brief background
   - What you have tried/thought of
   - Power to implement solution
   - Dream solution
   - Desired outcome of this meeting

3. **Springboards** Beginning thoughts/ideas on how to approach problem from problem owner + group, starting 'I wish...' or 'How to...'

4. **Selection** by problem owner on intrigue and appeal

   Does problem owner literally know how to do this? ◄───
   ⬇ No   Yes – go to Step 6

5. **Ways and Means** – Problem owner states intrigue and appeal, where needs help
   ⬇

   Specific and actionable ideas (6–12) from problem owner + group to deliver intrigue using action verbs ('What you do is...')
   ⬇

   Problem owner selects one/themed cluster ────────

6. **Emerging Idea** paraphrased in all detail by problem owner and written up ◄───
   ⬇

7. **Itemized Response** by problem owner listing pluses and one major concern starting 'Therefore I need a way to...'

   Collect ideas (6–8) to address the concern 'What you do is...'
   ⬇

   Problem owner selects one/several, modifying the Emerging Idea to create the Possible Solution

   Is problem owner at solution stage?
   ⬇ Yes – go to Step 8   No ────────

8. **Possible Solution** stated by problem owner, to original task with all modifications and written up
   ⬇

9. **Next Steps** actions listed by problem owner, what, by whom, by when

Getting ideas,

speculation,

dreaming and

new perspectives

Springboards

> *'Imagination is more important than knowledge.'*
>
> Albert Einstein

I introduced the cycling world's model earlier in the book. The innovation cycle for **doing** new things begins with speculation.

The birds flew around in the sky for years and years. One day, someone must have looked up and thought: 'That looks really great. **I wish I could do that.** It must be wonderful to be able to fly.'

Until someone had that thought and expressed a desire to do something that was clearly unrealistic at the time, it was not possible to have ideas that could lead to the innovation of a human flying like the birds.

Of course, people do not fly like birds; we use aeroplanes. The ideas behind the original thought gave us the solution, not the speculation itself.

Springboards are the beginning thoughts that lead us to new thinking.

Ideas are specific and actionable thoughts that allow us to move towards possible solutions.

'I know, I will flap my arms like the birds. No, that did not work… I know, I will fix banana leaves to my arms; they are like feathers. No, that does not work, but I am feeling a resistance against the air; let me continue to experiment…'

The **ideas** above are specific and actionable, not just speculative wishes.

Speculate when you need newness

Speculative thoughts, presented constructively, are labelled **'springboards'**.

You could liken them to the diving board in the swimming pool. At first, you may nervously step off the end. As you gain confidence you take leaps, and when you do not get hurt you may somersault as well.

So it is with speculation. As you enjoy the freedom of letting your mind roam free, see where it will take you, if you allow it space.

Springboards can include:

▨ redefinitions of the task headline;

▨ wishes;

▨ starting ideas;

▨ challenges to constraints on the problem;

▨ random thoughts;

▨ feelings or gut-level reactions;

▨ apparently conflicting points of view.

The purpose is to:

▨ open up the issue to new perspectives;

▨ increase the range of options;

▨ encourage speculation about future possibilities;

▨ maintain a positive climate;

▨ overcome the limiting effect of real-world restrictions;

▦ overcome the reluctance of non-experts to give ideas;

▦ overcome the tendency of experts to want to be right;

▦ encourage the use of speculative thinking.

Springboarding is turbocharged brainstorming.
   Normal judgement is suspended.
   Do not ask questions or allow them to be asked; encourage people to guess.
   Use **in–out listening** to hear everything spoken for what it suggests, not whether it is right or wrong.
   Practise suspending judgement in your thinking as well as your speaking – not an easy thing to do initially. It will take practice.
   Use **headlines** followed by **background** to express the spring-boards when working in a group.
   Capture the headlines on flipcharts so that the group can revel in their productivity.
   Use language like:

How to...
or
I wish...

Both of these formats encourage positive thinking about possible new futures.

If at first the idea is not absurd, then there is no hope for it

Albert Einstein

Imaging, metaphor, analogy and excursion – journeys into absurdity

The freedom to springboard will release some of the potential in people to have ideas and alternative perspectives.

Your mind is a very powerful tool and now I am going to describe ways to really stretch it.

To encourage the use of imaging, metaphor and analogy, the power that drives the turbocharger, use a process called **excursion**.

You will have had the experience many times in your life when something that you were unable to remember comes back to you at an apparently strange moment. Typically, this is when you are driving, showering, shaving, putting on make-up, sleeping etc. What is happening is that your subconscious is working on the problem that you were unable to solve, without you interfering, because you are now thinking about something else. When it has something to tell you, it does so.

Excursion is a process for capturing this effect whenever you wish.

There are many excursions and you can invent as many more as you wish. They share a common structure.

■ Do something to generate some thinking that is irrelevant to the problem you are trying to solve.

■ Allow this thinking to generate new springboards or ideas.

■ If you are using the excursion in the lower half of the process during idea development, use this material to invent absurd connections between the irrelevant material and the task.

If you think this sounds ridiculous, remember that judgement is suspended throughout this activity.

If you are still unsure, think about this. When doctors examined Einstein's brain after his death, they discovered it had many more synapses than a normal brain. It could make more connections faster than the average person. The suggestion is that this ability to make connections is how people are creative.

> *'You cannot solve a problem with the thinking that created it.'*
>
> Albert Einstein

Journey into absurdity

Why use absurdity?

- To expand the range of possibilities when addressing a problem or opportunity.

- To increase potential newness in the final ideas.

- To loosen the self-censor.

Characteristics of an absurd idea

Illegal	Impossible
Surprising	Fun
Unconventional	Illogical
Costs a lot	Once in a lifetime
Without conscience	Outrageous
Very risky	Shocking
Violates some basic laws of the universe, society or the company	Impractical

There are no rules about the right way to use absurd connections and ideas. They may have some element that directly addresses the problem – and they may have no connection at all!

Here are outline descriptions of some excursions, just to get you started.

Then go and invent some others for yourself. Some will work; others may not. It does not matter. There is no limit to how many you can use.

Imaging excursion

Additional ground rules:

1. Keep the image visual.

2. Keep it in one frame.

3. Keep yourself out.

▓ The facilitator gives the group a word, ideally having some ambiguity and not related to the issue.

▓ Do not write it down.

▓ Allow the group 5–10 seconds and then ask someone to describe his or her first thoughts as a picture, what he or she sees, not as a radio play.

▓ Get participants to add in their first thoughts in turn.

▓ Ask someone to make something extraordinary happen.

▓ Have the group make private notes as they replay the image created.

▓ Use this material to trigger additional speculation.

Career excursion

▓ Give each group member a career or role.

▓ Ask participants to make notes about thoughts that arise as they think themselves into the role.

█ Either:

  – Use this material directly to trigger new springboards.

  Or:

  –   Have each participant talk to the group about his or her
      thoughts to trigger additional material and then get new
      springboards.

█ A way to build on this if you want to have fun is to have the
   group play-act the roles when giving the springboards.

Outside excursion

█ Send the group outside and ask them to focus on something
   that intrigues or appeals to them.

█ Make notes about it and share this material on returning to the
   room to use as new triggers.

█ Alternatively, get participants to bring a range of objects back
   into the room and place them in a group in the middle as
   triggers.

█ A high-tech build is to give everyone a Polaroid camera and
   put the results on a wall, using this as trigger material.

Analogy excursion

█ Have the participants imagine becoming a part of an inan-
   imate or live object. Then ask them to describe how it feels and
   their relationship with others in the group.

█ Use the material to trigger new springboards.

Example excursion

▓ Ask the problem owner to identify the essence of the need in order to make progress.

▓ Ask the group to give you examples of this need from two worlds unrelated to the problem.

▓ List examples on a flip chart.

▓ Ask the group to use the examples to trigger new spring-boards.

For example, if the problem owner is saying, 'My key need is to get people working together who are currently not able to', we might suggest that it sounds like you are trying to create unlikely partnerships.

Therefore, get the group to list examples of unlikely partnerships in the worlds of 'nature' and 'theatre'. In nature, an example might be the birds that pick the crumbs out of the teeth of some animals.

So what are the attributes of this relationship, and how can they be connected with the problem under discussion to give new perspectives to thinking?

Evaluation

The quickest way

to stop progress

Selection is a key step in the process

and

needs to be given

a

high level of attention

Selection of springboards

You can generate springboards for as long as you wish. It is a lot of fun.

Judging when it is appropriate to stop is a matter of experience. However, the following guidelines will give you a place to start.

The problem owner decides when to move on to the next stage of the process, and may care to be guided in this by the feelings of the group.

There is no right or wrong time. You are engaged in generating a creative fog, so it is not a rational process capable of objective judgement.

Evaluation processes

Evaluation is an interesting part of the process of making progress. Often it is a subset of analysis paralysis. Particularly when seeking ideas in order to invent new ways of working on new things, be careful about evaluation.

I know of two processes in current use, labelled 'Stage-gates', and 'Funnels and Gates'. I am not passing a general opinion on these processes, and the names give a clue as to the intended use. Most of the companies using these that I have experienced use the **gate** as a barrier to shut down thinking.

Key performance indicators (KPIs) can be a useful way to focus on achievement of goals, assuming you have identified useful KPIs.

In the case of creativity and innovation, be aware that you may need to invent the measure as well. Until electricity was invented there wasn't this thing called a volt lying around to measure it. 'Ah, eureka, I have invented electricity; let me see how many volts it is!' No, this new phenomenon was so new that it was necessary to invent a new way to measure it.

I mentioned before how I often smile in new product development workshops when people are desperate to 'cluster' the new ideas. This usually means applying the existing segmentation to new thinking, whereupon a lot of the novelty is lost because the old assumptions and past experience get dragged in with the old label.

I offer some less traditional approaches to evaluation.

Be careful of assumptions; notice the word **ass-u-me**.

Selection based on intrigue

Many brainstorming sessions end with someone deciding to review all the ideas listed, turning them into a list of **good** and **bad** ideas. This is an objective and rational process. The **good** ideas are the ones that can be made sense of, so the label 'good' can be applied. The **bad** ideas are the ones that nobody can make sense of. As such, they contain all of the new thinking and are often rejected.

A rational selection is applied to the irrational process of **springboarding** and the result is that the very ideas that **might** lead to innovative possible solutions are rejected.

I could go along with the above process – but I would want to throw away the **good** ideas and work with the **bad**. My belief is that people are unable to use the bad ideas because they have no process for turning them into possible solutions.

I offer two key processes to allow you to use springboards:

▓   selection

and

▓   idea development

Select **springboards** based on what feels to be a high level of **intrigue**.

So what is this concept called *intrigue*?

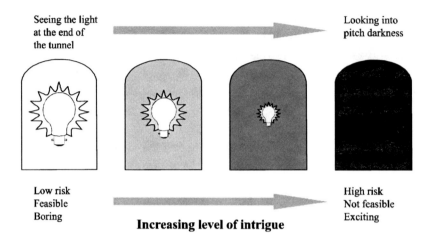

Imagine a tunnel on the left where you can see the light at the end of the tunnel. You know where it goes. It takes you to a known destination. This means it is a feasible journey, boring and unlikely to take you somewhere new. If you choose a **springboard** in this tunnel you are unlikely to innovate.

As the tunnels move to the right they become darker. On the right is a black hole that could lead somewhere exciting, or it may be a brick wall. You will never know unless you travel the path. **Springboards** in this tunnel are **intriguing**. They are exciting because they go into the unknown. It is risky, and the journey lacks feasibility because you do not know yet where you are going. This tunnel **may** lead you to new and innovative possible solutions.

Another way to conceptualize intrigue is to imagine a beach backed by limestone cliffs full of caves.

Think about when you were a child. Maybe you came across a shallow cave and you could squat inside it and imagine you were a shipwrecked sailor. Exciting for a while, but the game quickly becomes boring. Around the corner is a much deeper cave that disappears around a corner into the dark.

This is exciting!

You step inside and quickly it becomes dark and cold.

This is scary!

You step further in and can make out something in the back around the corner, a passage. Does it lead to the pirate's treasure, or are you going to step off a cliff and fall into a deep hole?

This is intriguing.

Intrigue is a vital step in the **creative** problem-solving process. Give time to allow review of the springboards and become intrigued. You have to play with the thoughts and let them develop. Intrigue sometimes just happens, and sometimes you need to let your mind mull things over for a while.

Idea development, a process map for using speculation and absurdity in order to generate new ways of working

Selection gave you a way to make choices from springboards. If you have chosen something intriguing, the chances are that it makes no sense in a rational world.

It is intriguing!

Idea development is the process that allows you to use the type of speculation generated during springboards and turn it into possible innovative solutions. This is a rational structured approach for taking irrational thoughts and raising the probability of turning these into useful action plans.

I use a metaphor to describe the **idea development** process. It is like catching snowflakes and creating snowballs. Each snowflake is unique and beautiful. If you simply clap your hands on to it, it will melt and you are left with nothing. In the beginning, you must treat the snowflakes gently and pat them into place, gradually creating a snowball. As it forms, it becomes more robust and you can begin to apply more pressure.

You can continue to add snowflakes for ever so your snowball has infinite size, and an infinite number of forms, as you choose where to add the next snowflakes. It will become as hard as glacial ice, very hard and very robust. Eventually, you could even choose to roll it down the mountain and let it have a life of its own.

If I continue the metaphor to include climate (remember the early chapters), then, as the climate changes, you will either have to continue to maintain the climate for a snowball, or let it go and begin again as the world moves on!

The role of the problem owner is to give direction to the group.

This is a key role at this point in the process. Unless the problem owner is able to give direction to the group, the group members will have no way to generate further ideas. Without direction from the problem owner, the group will be left floundering in the creative fog with no way out.

Idea development is often tough, like swimming through treacle with your hands tied behind your back.

The key steps are:

▨ Work with one springboard at a time – you can always go back and try others later.

▨ The problem owner talks to the group about the intrigue, and the group uses **in–out listening** to trigger specific and actionable ideas that would deliver the intrigue.

Specific and actionable ideas use a headline format like:

What you do is…

This is different from wishing, which is speculative. You have expanded your thinking to the maximum width of the kite, made a selection and now you are going to begin **gradually to introduce feasibility**:

1. The group generates a series of specific and actionable ideas, fewer of them than for springboards. The problem owner should join in and give ideas as well.

2. Stop after a while and invite the problem owner to consider the ideas to see if **one or more of them is beginning to suggest a**

concept or direction of thinking that could be pursued further.

3. If not, continue to get more ideas. Use an **excursion** if you wish to keep the thinking open-minded.

4. If yes, get the problem owner to use an **itemized response** (see following pages) to identify the pluses, and one major concern. (Work through one concern at a time. The danger of raising too many concerns too soon for a beginning idea is that the group becomes so de-energized that its members give up hope.)

5. Collect ideas to address the concern and then go back to the problem owner and repeat the process from step 2.

6. Keep cycling through the process until you get to a solution, or decide it is going nowhere and try another springboard.

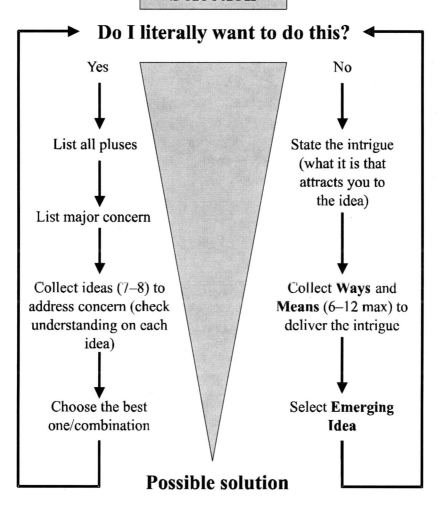

Selection

Do I literally want to do this?

Yes   No

List all pluses

List major concern

Collect ideas (7–8) to
address concern (check
understanding on each
idea)

Choose the best
one/combination

State the intrigue
(what it is that
attracts you to
the idea)

Collect **Ways** and
Means (6–12 max) to
deliver the intrigue

Select **Emerging
Idea**

Possible solution

Take the following example.

My problem is: **How to keep the office quieter**.

The springboard I have chosen is: **I wish you could stop James from talking so loudly**.

A specific and actionable idea to address this is: **What you do is cut his head off**.

This would solve my problem.

List all the pluses for this idea. There are many – for example: I like the speed and finality of this suggestion.

My major concern is: **How to do this without getting arrested**. I need a way to have the effect of cutting a head off without actually doing it. Give me some further ideas:

Put a muzzle on him.
Tape his mouth up.
Staple his lips together.

These are looking good, and they will all solve the problem.

I like the muzzling of sound concept. My major concern is: **How to muzzle him in a less antisocial way**:

Put him in a separate office.
Use soundproof screens.
Install white-noise generators tuned to James.

This is a contrived illustration to try and get a difficult concept across. You will see how a ludicrous suggestion like cutting a head off, treated positively using an **itemized response**, can be used to generate more feasible ideas.

Risk taking

Consider the phrase introduced in **being** – 'There is no failure, only feedback.' The risk of feedback is very low; the risk of failure is very high. If you see results as failures, you may create a **programme** in yourself that leads to fear of failure.

The world moves on. You can either travel with it or be left behind. In order to travel, you will have to do new things. Risk is a part of life. Just as **you cannot not influence** and cannot not communicate, so you **cannot not take risks.**

The issue is how to measure risk and make useful decisions that give you the possibility of achieving the outcome you are looking for. Particularly in the context of creativity and innovation, **doing** new things may mean working on **'gut feel'** for a while. Notice the words **'gut'** and **'feel'**.

If you turn back to the figure earlier in the book describing subjective experience, you will see a picture of a system where all the parts affect every other part.

My belief is that a **gut feel** is an evaluation made by your subconscious that you are currently unable to put words to. It is a conclusion reached in your **deep structure** for which you have not yet found **a surface-structure** label. Sometimes this is called **intuition.** 'Trust your feelings' is a phrase you will have heard. Some great decisions have been made on this basis. The Sony Walkman failed in market research and the decision was made to go for it: the rest is history.

I do not have any tidy suggestions for how you measure risk. I do not think there are any tidy answers. I wrote earlier that life is a messy business. Many people find themselves believing they have found the **'truth'** of a situation by assigning a clarity to it based upon measures that may or may not be yielding useful information.

When you find measures that are clearly **right** for a situation, please go ahead and use them. These measures exist to some extent of course. **Also**, be prepared to throw them away sometimes, and trust to your feelings. Get creative about how you measure. I know a company that checked morale by counting how many people were smiling in the office. It proved to be a useful measure.

Here is a matrix for measuring risk.

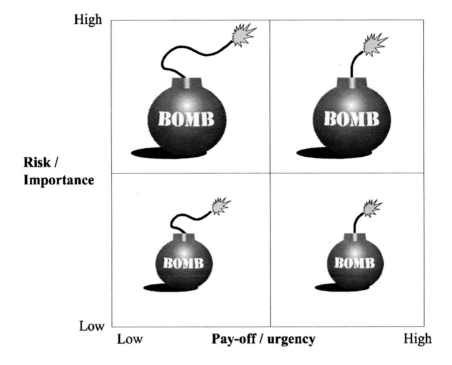

For any task or set of data, assign items to the boxes. Large bombs on short fuses, when defused, give you the bigger pay-off, either from avoiding the explosion, or in the resource you have now saved from destroying itself, depending upon your point of view. A matrix like this forces you to ask questions of yourself rather like those introduced earlier. It forces you to be specific and, in being specific, you often find those things for which meaningful measures exist, and those areas where you are fooling yourself.

I think it is correct to write that **all** research on innovation says companies that are risk-averse tend to be less innovative. Nobody should be surprised at this; it is obvious. As a leader, **be** open and honest about your own fears of failure for yourself and your company; we all have such fears.

The positive intention of the fear is to protect us from destruction. Knowing this can free you to recognize when it is OK to take the risks. Just as with influencing and communicating, you can then make choices about the risks to take, rather than being a rabbit in the headlights and waiting for the world to splatter you and your company all over the road.

Itemized response

Itemized response is a process for protecting ideas.

Think about how you respond to new ideas or opinions offered to you, and how others respond when you make the offers.

Speculation and new ideas are like babies, easily hurt and destroyed unless you protect them. Given the right environment within which to grow and develop, stunning results can be achieved.

Often groups evaluate ideas by saying only what is wrong, and the level of criticism or evaluation is so general that it is useless as a guide as to how to improve the thinking.

The **itemized response** process itemizes, as a series of headlines, the evaluation of an idea or set of circumstances.

You begin by **listing the pluses,** or positive aspects, of the idea. Many times, potentially valuable thinking is never recognized as such because sufficient time is not given to working through the pluses for the idea. Listing pluses is, in itself, a building process. Using **in–out listening,** additional pluses will be triggered and suddenly an idea can blossom.

After the pluses have been listed, move on to look at the **areas of concern** that need to be addressed – do not think of it as what is wrong. List these as headlines using a problem-solving focus like:

■ **How to...**

■ **I wish...**

■ **I need a way...**

This form of words establishes what needs to happen for the idea to improve, and sets you up with problem-solving statements to work with creatively.

If you believe something is too expensive and simply say so – 'It is too expensive!' – this leaves very limited options for where to go next. 'Too expensive' is a shut-out. Many members of the group will simply stop thinking about implementing the idea.

Turning this into a more positive focus will dramatically change the perspective of the group.

Maybe you are thinking, 'I like the solution **and** my issue is…'

▓ '… how to do this with cheaper raw materials.'

▓ '… how to use different budgets.'

▓ '… I need a way to do this over two years.'

▓ '… I wish we could find cheaper labour.'

All of these statements are versions of 'too expensive'-type thinking. They are more specific, however, and we can now address the issues using creative problem solving.

Try listing all the things wrong with the original ring-pull can as a retail drinks packaging concept. You will manage to generate a long list of its faults, some apparently real show-stoppers – you drink from a dirty surface, it is not resealable and children can cut themselves, for example. You could be forgiven for wondering why the concept was even launched. This was one of the most successful packaging concepts launched for years, yet if you bother to look at why it won't work it is easy to kill the idea off.

So many companies fail to act because they scare themselves to death and never make the decision – analysis paralysis again.

When looking at concerns, differentiate between **major** and **minor** concerns.

I once watched a 14-person executive team make a decision. I was videotaping the meeting as a training process. The problem owner had made a difficult decision, helped by his colleagues. It was an important decision for the business and clearly a good decision. Everybody looked pleased and energetic, especially the problem owner. Great! The group decided to use an **itemized response** to check on the decision, and the information from it would be useful for communicating the decision. Again, this seemed like a good idea. They generated four flipcharts of headlines describing the positive features of the decision and everybody was looking even happier. OK so far!

The facilitator asked for issues or concerns. Clearly, there were none of any significance as there was silence. Then somebody offered a small concern. It was a nit-picking concern that would have no consequence for the decision to be implemented. However, it was noted, and somebody then raised another nit-picking concern. This opened the floodgates and a series of nit-picking issues were voiced.

As the list grew, I was watching the energy in the group go down. The problem owner was visibly shrinking lower in his seat. I stopped the process before it became more damaging. I showed the group themselves on the video and asked them what they were doing. Lots of sheepish grins around the table. Again their concern was not contributing usefully to the outcome of the meeting; indeed it was positively damaging it.

I think it is important to differentiate between **major concerns**, ie show-stoppers, and **minor concerns**, ie issues that stop the idea or decision being perfect and do not **have** to be resolved to allow the decision to go forward. So many companies talk themselves into an almost catatonic state of immobility by talking **down** proposals and decisions so nothing ever happens. Remember the ring-pull can.

Best current thinking

This is a construct for managing the confusion that often arises between:

- opinions;

- facts;

- ideas;

- decisions.

How often have you been on the receiving end of someone giving you his or her opinion with such ferocity and enthusiasm that it sounds like the person is telling you that is the way things are, incontrovertibly? Someone who is so enthusiastic about an opinion can get so energetic about sharing it that the intended effect is lost as he or she almost physically pushes the listener into the corner of the room. It is hard to hear an **opinion** if it sounds like a **fact** and you have a different view. I am not sure there are many **facts** in the world.

The *Oxford English Dictionary* assigns the words **'truth'** and **'reality'** to the definition of **'fact'**. Many times, **facts** are actually a current situation that can be changed, so it is a **policy** or **current practice**. This does not make a fact. Many successful **facts** have been completely overturned, flat world to round for a start. Auditors' statements are explicit that it is an **opinion** about the company, because any set of figures is only one view of the business, and many others could be generated if someone chose to do so.

By being specific about the point you are making, a lot of arguments can be avoided.

Ideas and **decisions** often give rise to a similar confusion. Sometimes people describe an **idea** in such a way that it sounds like a **decision** has been made. If you disagree with what you are hearing and you are thinking of it as a **decision** it will be very hard to maintain your concentration on genuinely hearing the **idea**. (This is a good example of where the 'positive intention' that you read about earlier would be helpful.)

Best current thinking, by definition, is a statement or proposal of an idea or opinion, or set of ideas and opinions. Some elements of the proposal may be fixed because nobody has the power to change that element – maybe a law that is not worth challenging in the short run, for example. Other elements may be changeable. By being specific about this, time can be spent where it is useful, where change can be made. It also saves time arguing about issues that cannot be changed, damaging the climate of your group with unnecessary conflict.

Best current thinking, by definition, can be modified and changed. This means it is easier to hear, particularly in a situation where views that conflict exist. Providing I know my **opinions** will be heard and I have an opportunity to modify a proposal, I am more likely to listen attentively to the argued proposal.

Best current thinking generates more open supportive climates, with high levels of listening and understanding. This is useful for a leader who is trying to share a message and win commitment to achieving outcomes. (A structure for a meeting geared to best current thinking is in Appendix 1.)

Comfort rating

Those of you who still want to see some numbers will like this. A comfort rating is a quick way to evaluate a proposal or decision. It is a score of 1 to 10, where 10 is very comfortable and 1 is 'I think it has no value at all.' Everyone in a group, whose opinion we wish to hear, is asked to write down privately his or her score after listening to a proposal. This avoids dominoes. If the boss gives it a score publicly first, it is a strong team that is prepared to disagree.

Once the scores are written down, they are collected. The rules are that a score of 7 defines a level of acceptability. If you score 7 or greater, it means you are prepared to go with the proposal as it stands and only have minor concerns. A score of 6 or less means you have a major concern that has to be resolved before you are prepared to support the proposal.

Bear in mind the concept of problem ownership as you read this. It is OK in my view for a problem owner to hear concerns and then say, 'Fine, I understand these and I am still making my decision.' There will be consequences, of course, and they will have to be managed. Leaders have to make decisions. Consensus is not always possible or even desirable. Decide your outcome and behave flexibly to achieve this!

After completing the comfort rating, if there are any concerns use an itemized response. Collect all pluses first. For people who plan to raise a major concern it can be useful to raise pluses first, as the concern is more likely to be listened to. Collect concerns with headlines beginning 'I wish…', 'How to…' or 'I need a way to…' This form of words establishes what needs to happen for the idea to improve, and sets you up with problem-solving statements to work with creatively.

Next steps

Next steps are a part of the evaluation process. They mark that you have finished the particular activity

Finish with some next steps

otherwise

why bother to make the effort?

Ensure every action has

a name and

a time on it

Appendix 1

Structures for group working

I think that there are only four meeting structures in the world. All meetings are a version of these. The structures are described in the next few pages.

Decision-making styles

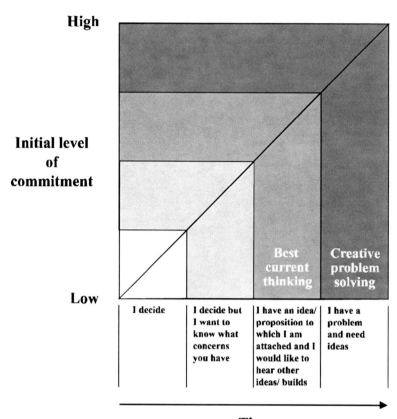

Guidelines for making decisions

1. Be sure you can carry it through.
2. Give people a chance to hear/understand why you are making this choice.
3. Work hard to build commitment later and continue with this. You cannot assume commitment is a steady state.

'**I decide**' has the benefit of speed, the downside being typically low levels of commitment from others.

'**I decide but I want to know what concerns you have**' takes a little longer. Providing you genuinely listen to people's concerns and are believed to have done so, you will get more commitment.

'**I have an idea and would like your help to build it into a solution' (best current thinking)** takes even longer and gives you much higher levels of commitment to the decision.

'**I have a problem and I need ideas' (creative problem solving)** takes longest of all and will get you a much higher level of commitment to the outcome.

None of these is the right or wrong way. The opportunity is to make an appropriate choice. If your child is about to run under a bus, I suggest you make an instant decision, tell him/her and accompany this with instant action. Even if you break the child's arm, it will still be better than the likely alternative.

It is also worth considering the way we measure time (and money). One of my clients historically brought new products to market by having a series of people work together in different teams over a period of months or years, a typical sequential project approach. Maybe marketing have the first ideas, research teams test the ideas, labs invent some things, manufacturing eventually get involved etc. We ran a three-day meeting that involved all of the parties who would become involved over time, including consumers. At the end of this, the client had numerous breakthrough ideas to take to market and great enthusiasm and high levels of commitment from all who participated. He reckoned he had done the equivalent of nine months' work in three days.

Now, how much longer does it take to use creative problem solving!

Armed with the tools and the structures, you can bring together diverse groups to work in this way as well.

Backward/forward planning

This is a planning tool based upon chunking that was introduced earlier. It is designed to help you sort out what the real issue is you may wish to work on, often not easy to do in complex confusing organizations. Knowing the task you wish to work on also allows you properly to identify the problem owner. In turn, this tells you who to involve in the meeting, who not to involve and the type of meeting you should design.

Steps – 'backward'

a   Form a starting 'How to...' headline and write it down in the centre of the page.

b   Ask the question: 'Imagine you have now solved this problem...' (cover up the 'How to' part of the headline and turn the problem statement into a solution) and then ask, 'What problem does that resolve for you?', and write the answer down as a 'How to...' headline.

c   With this new 'How to...' headline, ask the question again: 'Imagine you have now solved this problem, what problem does that resolve for you?' Again, write down the answer as a 'How to...' headline.

d   Use this process twice more so that you now have five 'How to...' headlines.

Steps – 'forward'

e   Go back to your original headline and ask the question: 'Imagine you have now solved this problem; what else could it give you?' or 'What more could you have?' or 'What other benefits are there?' List at least three. They need to be different from the 'backward' headlines.

f   Put 'How to…' in front of each of the benefits. You now have eight headlines.

g   The final question is a confronting question. Go back again to the original headline and ask: 'What is stopping you from making it happen? Why haven't you solved it?', and write the answer down as a 'How to…' headline.

h   Now look through the nine headlines and decide which is the most appropriate starting point. It may be the original headline and that is fine, as it will be chosen with some perspective.

Nine-Step Synectics Problem Solving Process

1. **Task Headline** from problem owner starting 'How to...'

2. **Task Analysis** from problem owner stating:
   - Why problem/opportunity
   - Brief background
   - What you have tried/thought of
   - Power to implement solution
   - Dream solution
   - Desired outcome of this meeting

3. **Springboards** Beginning thoughts/ideas on how to approach problem from problem owner + group, starting 'I wish...' or 'How to...'

4. **Selection** by problem owner on intrigue and appeal

   Does problem owner literally know how to do this?
   ⬇ No   Yes – go to Step 6

5. **Ways and Means** – Problem owner states intrigue and appeal, where needs help
   ⬇
   Specific and actionable ideas (6–12) from problem owner + group
   to deliver intrigue using action verbs ('What you do is...')
   ⬇
   Problem owner selects one/themed cluster

6. **Emerging Idea** paraphrased in all detail by problem owner and written up ⬅
   ⬇

7. **Itemized Response** by problem owner listing pluses and one major concern starting 'Therefore I need a way to...'
   ⬇
   Collect ideas (6–8) to address the concern 'What you do is...'
   ⬇
   Problem owner selects one/several, modifying the Emerging Idea
   to create the Possible Solution

   Is problem owner at solution stage?
   ⬇ Yes – go to Step 8   No

8. **Possible Solution** stated by problem owner, to original task with all modifications and written up
   ⬇

9. **Next Steps** actions listed by problem owner, what, by whom, by when

Synectics Creative Problem-Solving Process flow chart

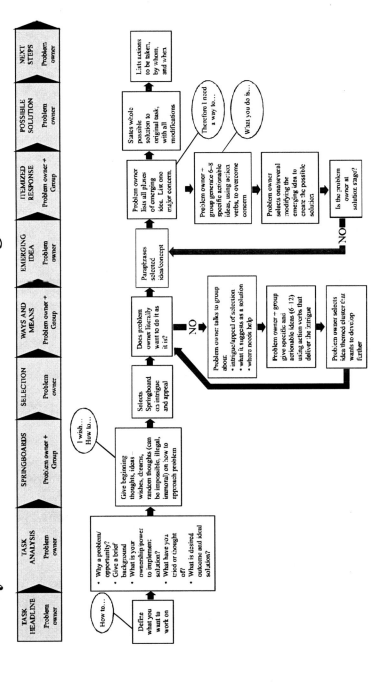

Best current thinking

This is appropriate when you have a proposed solution that involves other people in its implementation. That is, you have a solution; other people have some or all of the responsibility for action.

Sharing intention and winning commitment

▓ **Present your proposal/suggestion to those involved.**
- State how fixed it is (to what extent can it be modified by the group?).

▓ **Check they understand it.**
- Take questions for clarification.
- Ask people to paraphrase key parts.

▓ **Evaluate it open-mindedly (maybe preceded by a comfort rating).**
- Everyone lists all possible benefits for the suggestion.
- Everyone lists the problems or concerns they have, particularly where it affects them personally.

▓ **Set priorities on the concerns.**
- Everyone selects two concerns they think are the most important to resolve first.

▓ **Take each concern in turn and problem-solve it.**
- Ownership passes to the person who raised the concern. (This is to avoid someone sitting in the meeting raising concerns for others to work on. Finally, ownership returns to the ultimate owner of the meeting.)
- The new problem owner, with the group's help, generates and develops ideas until the concern is resolved.

▓ **Modify or add to the original proposal.**
- To take account of the new ideas.
- Making sure that you (the original client) are still comfortable with the overall proposal.

▓ **Repeat until the major concerns are resolved and the modified proposal meets everybody's needs.**

The Synectics agenda meeting

Main features

▧ Separate process facilitator (where possible).

▧ Agenda written up at meeting.

▧ Minutes visibly written up at meeting.

▧ Each item is owned by a problem owner.

▧ Items are dealt with one at a time, each owner in turn.

▧ The purpose of each item is explicit.

▧ Time:
   – Overall time is set; meeting starts and finishes on time.
   – Time taken for each item is estimated and the actual time taken is recorded.

Example agenda

Owner Name	Item Name	Purpose and Process	Time	
			Estimated	Actual
Chris	Project X Budgets Sales targets	Information get Problem solve Information give	10 mins 7 mins 3 mins	
Geoff	Sales figures Project X	Information give Problem solve	5 mins 10 mins	
Hilary	Training Recruitment Salaries New personnel	Problem solve Information get Problem solve Information give	10 mins 8 mins 10 mins 4 mins	
Margaret	Project X	Information give	5 mins	

This meeting format applies some of the principles of the Synectics creative problem-solving meeting to other meetings with a mixed agenda, for example the regular meetings of executive committees, project reviews, planning meetings.

1. Features

The main features of the Synectics agenda meeting:

1.1 Process facilitator

A process facilitator who takes no part in the content of the meeting runs the meeting. A clear distinction is maintained between 'process' and 'content'; the facilitator has authority over process only. The facilitator also carries out some of the administrative and recording duties often performed by a committee secretary.

1.2 'Problem owner' role

Every item on the agenda is associated by name with the person who raised it. Thus at all times the group knows for whom they are working. The same subject may be raised by several individuals and is treated as several distinct items. One agenda item is dealt with for each person in sequence followed by further cycles. Members of the meeting may add new agenda items to their list at any time during the meeting.

1.3 Purpose

For each item, the owner must specify the purpose for which he/she has raised it so that the group will know what is wanted from them. In practice, there seem to be only four purposes for which any item is raised:
- give information;
- get information;
- solve a problem;
- make a decision.

1.4 Time

The duration of the meeting is fixed in advance and can be extended only by unanimous consent. The time spent on each item is recorded (visibly) against the name of the individual who raised it, so that at the end of the meeting it is apparent how the total time has been taken up by each individual on the items raised.

A time limit is also set for each item. Giving and getting information on any individual item can normally be accomplished in less than 10 minutes; if more than 10 minutes is required, other forms of communication report, presentation or lecture may be more effective.

Problem solving may well require more than 30 minutes, in which case a special problem-solving meeting is set up outside the agenda meeting. The membership of the problem-solving meeting is tailored to the problem and may well be different from that of the agenda meeting.

1.5 Visible recording

The facilitator writes up on large pads:
- The agenda items against the name of the individual who raises them.
- The time spent on each item.
- 'Minutes' to the extent that the 'problem owner' for each item asks for a record to be made. We recommend recording all action steps, in the words of the person who is responsible for taking the action. All decisions and new agreements should also be written up on the flipcharts.

2. Meeting structure

The structure of the meeting is as follows:

2.1　Process facilitator is appointed from outside the meeting.

2.2　Facilitator fixes time, place, duration and obtains from participants a preliminary indication of likely agenda; agrees time limit per item; generally 'plans' the meeting.

2.3　Meeting starts on time.

2.4　Facilitator asks participants for their agenda items (key words) and writes up on large pads.

2.5　Facilitator decides rotation and starts with first 'problem owner', who chooses item from his/her list.

2.6 Facilitator asks the problem owner what the group should listen for, ie whether the purpose of the item is giving/getting information or problem solving.

2.7 At the end of the item, or when time limit is reached, the facilitator records time spent on it and any conclusion/action steps the 'problem owner' wants is written on the flipchart.

2.8 Facilitator goes to other problem owners in sequence and repeats cycle.

2.9 Ten minutes from the end, facilitator may ask group whether they wish to extend time or give priority to a particular item.

2.10 Meeting closes at the scheduled (or extended) time as agreed; items left over can be raised at the next meeting or dealt with outside the meeting.

3. Benefits

3.1 Efficient use of time. Items requiring longer time are delegated to a separate meeting with suitable membership for that item.

3.2 Clarification of responsibility for and purpose of each item.

3.3 Efficient conduct of the meeting without manipulation. Power and authority are applied to the process, not to the content, by an independent leader.

3.4 Minutes are written publicly and can be corrected at the time, if necessary.

Decision making

Some pointers

Appropriate when there are a number of options that could be developed and pursued.

Objective is to agree on the priority of one or more options to take forward, judged against agreed criteria.

Key principles

▓ List the options.

▓ Evaluate each one constructively by listing its pluses and concerns.

▓ Generate ways to overcome the key concerns.

Additional processes

▓ Agree criteria first, the 'musts' from the 'nice ifs'.

▓ Generate options.

▓ Match new and existing options to the criteria.

▓ Agree priorities (eg by looking at risk/pay-off).

These processes are particularly appropriate when a number of people need to agree on the decision, and when there are potentially a large number of options (eg when deciding which R & D routes to pursue or which markets to develop).

One of the important features of this process is the inclusion of creative problem-solving skills at key stages in the process. These skills can significantly increase the quality of decisions by increasing options and in helping develop options before making a decision. A key element in this process is first to establish who will make the decision, and the role of the rest of the team.

Other steps are set out below.

Step 1   Outline meeting objective

▨ What is the decision to be made?

▨ To what final state of affairs do I wish this decision to take me?

▨ To what extent is a creative as opposed to a routine approach critical to the success of this project?

Step 2   Establish decision criteria

Often in a decision-making process, key options will be considered before the criteria on which the decision will be based are considered.

Having explicit criteria makes it easier to find ways of reconciling the different needs of those involved. This is because the values that are driving the choices are out in the open. There are often creative ways of meeting apparently contradictory criteria.

Step 3   Generate options

Often a group will have focused quickly on a couple of alternatives without considering what other options are available. This step in the process enables additional alternatives to be generated before finally closing. The idea-generation skills covered in the previous section, in particular the 'no evaluation' ground rules, will be useful at this stage.

Step 4   Prioritize and choose against criteria

Once the additional alternatives have been listed, the group makes a selection of their preferred options. These may not have changed significantly.

Step 5   Structured evaluation of key options

The key options are evaluated in a structured way. The group specifies all the positive features of an option before listing the negative aspects as directions for improvement, using the phrases:

'How to...'
'I need to find a way to...'

These concerns are numbered and the group then chooses those concerns that must be overcome before the option is acted upon. A group selection matrix may be useful at this stage.

This step in the process is an important one in terms of capturing the 'intuitions/hunches' on which evaluation will be based. Furthermore, if they have been recorded, they can be referred back to at a later date as a means of refining the intuitive basis of decision.

Step 6   Problem-solve around key concerns

The key concerns are taken one at a time and used as a task headline for further idea generation until the concern has been overcome and a decision becomes apparent.

Step 7   Risk/pay-off matrix

Prior to making a final decision it is worth establishing where the options are in terms of risk/pay-off (the bomb diagram you read about earlier).

Appendix 2: Communication for managing conflict

Many people are conflict-averse. Synectics processes are designed to avoid conflict deliberately by working in previously agreed structures and agreeing to certain rules. This is useful on many occasions. However, it does not mean we can simply ignore conflict and hope it will go away.

Conflict means there is energy and this is to be welcomed. The challenge is how to harness the energy positively. The following is a construct for managing conflict taken from work by Ben Fuchs, a conflict facilitator who works with large groups using a similar construct. If you are operating in the role of facilitator, as with any coaching intervention it is important to get the permission of people you are working with before applying the model. If you are one of the parties in a conflict, you may choose to suggest formally that the model is used.

Alternatively, try using the model slipped into normal conversation as a way of influencing the structure of the interaction in order to get a more constructive outcome. Offer your side of the 'argument' using the language construct, and offer your 'opponent' the opportunity to do the same and see what changes.

Differentiating between inner and outer experiences

Inner map 1	Outer experience	Inner map 2

'The map is not the territory'

Words
Tones
Non-verbals

Picture		Picture
Sound		Sound
Feeling		Feeling
Taste		Taste
Smell		Smell
Self-talk		Self-talk

| INTERNAL STATE | | INTERNAL STATE |

Words
Tones
Non-verbals

Feelings		Feelings
Sensations		Sensations
Physiology		Physiology
Emotions		Emotions

Perceptual filters – 1	Perceptual filters – 2
Beliefs	Beliefs
Values	Values
Past experiences	Past experiences

Differentiating is an important skill in articulating our experiences – differentiating 'inner' from 'outer' experience. The outer experience is what the other person's actual behaviour is. If a person were videotaped doing something, most people would be able to describe the same behaviour. But their interpretations of that behaviour and its motivations would differ.

The 'inner' experience is what we do inside ourselves with that behaviour – how we interpret it, what motivations we ascribe to it, etc. Here, we can further differentiate between our thoughts (what we imagine and interpret from the behaviour), our feelings (our emotional reactions to that information) and our intentions (what we want or are trying to do).

The following model helps to differentiate.

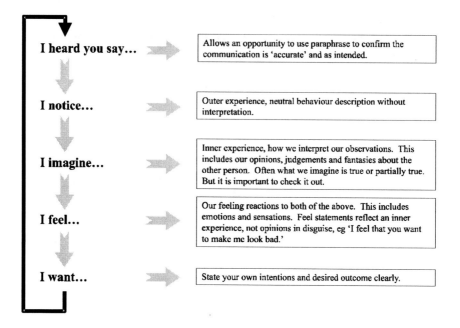

I heard you say... → Allows an opportunity to use paraphrase to confirm the communication is 'accurate' and as intended.

I notice... → Outer experience, neutral behaviour description without interpretation.

I imagine... → Inner experience, how we interpret our observations. This includes our opinions, judgements and fantasies about the other person. Often what we imagine is true or partially true. But it is important to check it out.

I feel... → Our feeling reactions to both of the above. This includes emotions and sensations. Feel statements reflect an inner experience, not opinions in disguise, eg 'I feel that you want to make me look bad.'

I want... → State your own intentions and desired outcome clearly.

Defensive communication

I'm on a win–lose with you and will not give away anything that you could use against me. I look for opportunities to score points and to win. I will listen to you just enough to gather ammunition to win the argument, but am not interested in your experience as a person. Key features are: fear (unacknowledged), blaming, competing for moral high ground, avoiding guilt and shame, proving yourself right.

Collaborative communication

I am looking for a win–win with you. I can tell you how it is for me because I want you to understand me better. I will listen to you because I want to know how it is for you. Listening does not mean agreeing, simply understanding where you are 'coming from'. Key features are: compassion, trust, willingness to admit mistakes, vulnerability, putting relationship and learning above being right.

Appendix 3:
Synectics and its origins

Forty years ago, two people in a design invention team became curious about why it was that on some days they had productive ideas sessions and on others the group argued a lot and went round in circles. They began to videotape the meetings and review the behaviour of the group. They noticed recurring behaviours, some very useful and constructive, others very destructive.

The decision was made to try to change how they organized and behaved in meetings, doing more of the constructive things and finding new ways of managing the destructive behaviour. They were successful and became more effective by their measures. The two guys also began to wonder if they could make creativity and innovation more than just an 'accident'.

They set up a new company called **Synectics**. The word was derived from the Greek **'syn' – the bringing together of diverse elements** – and **'ectos' – from outside**. A company was formed that has also given birth to a growing body of knowledge, because Synectics is also the name for the set of tools and techniques.

From continued observation of invention and design sessions, Synectics have developed a set of tools and structures. These model and allow people to raise the probability of successfully using the processes of having ideas, being creative, making choices when looking for new ways of working, and developing new solutions from the kind of woolly stuff you get when people are speculating about possible futures.

These tools and processes are used in many major international firms across the globe.

Appendix 4: What is NLP?

Neuro-Linguistic Programming (NLP) has many strengths, but a clear and helpful name isn't one of them! Fortunately, it can be defined straightforwardly as *the study of excellence.*

Overview

NLP was born when John Grinder, a linguist, and Richard Bandler, a mathematician, asked themselves a simple yet fascinating question. What is it that makes the difference between somebody who is merely competent at any given skill and somebody who *excels* at the same skill.

People typically answer that question in one of two ways: either that some people have natural gifts or talents for a particular skill, or that practice and experience are what count.

NLP side-steps these answers by focusing not on what has made the difference in the past between two people of different abilities, but on what can be done now to turn the competent person's performance into one of excellence.

NLP proposes that there are three elements to any skill or behaviour. First, there is the external behaviour, that is, what the person actually does and says. Second, there is the person's internal computation, that is, what the person thinks and the way in which he or she thinks. And third, there is the person's internal state, that is, what and how the person feels.

Each of these three elements can be examined in detail. A movement, for example, can be reduced to the level of micro-muscle movements. An internal image can be defined by size, position, colour, contrast and so on. An internal voice can be defined by the words themselves, tone of voice, volume, location and similar. A feeling can be described by position, intensity, temperature, direction of movement.

Modelling

By following this process, it is possible to build up an extremely comprehensive model of any excellent behaviour. This model of excellence can then be acquired by the competent person simply by reversing the process; the competent person makes the same movements, images, voices, feelings.

In some cases, we may need to expand our model to include such things as beliefs and what NLP calls 'perceptual filters': the ways in which our past experiences affect the way we now perceive the world.

Modelling need not involve someone else. It is equally possible to model yourself. Suppose, for example, that you feel nervous when you have to speak to a large group of people. Instead of finding someone who is a confident public speaker and modelling him or her, you could simply find a different situation in which you feel confident (perhaps talking to two or three people) and model yourself in that context.

NLP is the name given to a set of tools, techniques and approaches used to carry out this transformation.

The type of modelling we have described has long been applied to the objective world. Most of the science we now call 'engineering', for example, came about by people studying what worked in natural structures, working out the principles involved and then applying those same principles to new structures.

NLP simply applies the same process to excellence in people. It studies the underlying structures of the skills, behaviours and experiences of excellence, and then assists people in using those structures effectively. Thus NLP is sometimes defined as *the study of the structure of subjective experience.*

Applications

NLP has been successfully applied to the fields of business, sport, therapy, education and the performing arts. The tools it offers can be applied equally well to any human activity.

In modelling examples of excellence in fields as diverse as hypnotherapy, tennis, training, acting and team management, NLP has also developed a number of specific models of excellence that are now considered part of NLP. Examples include a highly successful phobia cure, an elegant format for resolving internal conflict, and an impressive format for running streamlined meetings. These models are typically taught as part of NLP training programmes.

Presuppositions

The work done using NLP has also resulted in a number of attitudes or presuppositions that seem to be useful when aiming for excellence. Note that NLP doesn't claim that these presuppositions are true, merely that it is useful to behave as if they are.

The distinction is an important one. NLP doesn't insist that you change your beliefs about the world, merely that you be prepared to experiment with other approaches. It's rather like catching a train to an important meeting; it may not be true that railway timetables are unreliable but – if it is important to be at the meeting on time – it might be useful to behave as if they are and phone first to check that the train is running. Among the presuppositions normally presented on NLP training are:

▓ **The map is not the territory.**
In other words, the description of an experience is not the same as the experience itself. We live in a world in which we pay a good deal of attention to words. We often behave as if words were a direct and undeniably accurate description of experience. NLP invites us to make a distinction between the words and the experience they describe.

▓ **Choice is always better than no choice.**
Most of us have an understandable tendency, when we succeed in something, to view our successful approach as the 'right' approach to use in future. NLP suggests that, even when we have behaviours that work perfectly, it is still useful to have other options: to be able to choose from several successful behaviours. That way, if one of them turns out not to work, we have other successful behaviours to call on.

▓ **There is no failure, only feedback.**
When things don't work out the way we'd hoped they would, a common response is to consider that we 'failed'. NLP offers an alternative view: that what actually happened is neither good nor bad but merely information. Think back to when you learnt to drive. You almost certainly crunched the gears at some point. That didn't mean that you failed as a driver and would never be able to operate the gearbox; it simply meant that changing gear in that particular way didn't produce the result you wanted. You then used that information to improve the way you changed gears.

▓ **The meaning of the communication is the response it produces.**
This follows on from the previous presupposition. If our communications don't produce the responses we would like, we can either decide that the other person is to 'blame' for not responding appropriately or we can simply accept that our communication produced the result it did and decide what we would like to do now. The first approach leaves us powerless:

we are in the hands of the other person. The latter approach enables us to treat the response as information and change our behaviour accordingly. This places us in the powerful position of a flexible communicator willing to take responsibility for achieving things we would like. (We use the word 'responsibility' in its literal sense – the ability to respond.)

Behavioural flexibility

You'll hear quite a lot in NLP about three ways of doing things. NLP takes the view that one option is (obviously) no choice at all, two options are a dilemma and that choice only begins when you have at least three approaches. Having at least three powerful approaches to any goal, and being willing to use whichever option is most appropriate at the time, is what NLP refers to as behavioural flexibility.

One of the most powerful forms of behavioural flexibility is what NLP calls first-, second- and third-person shifts.

When we are experiencing things through our own eyes and ears, we are said to be associated, or in the first person. If we now wonder how someone else is experiencing something and 'put ourselves in the other person's shoes', we are said to be in the second person; and if we see and hear both ourself and the other people as if we were an observer, we are said to be disassociated or in the third person.

We all switch between first, second and third person quite naturally, often without really being aware that we are doing it. NLP teaches the skill of deliberately shifting consciousness in this way to gather information – to see things literally from another person's point of view.

That name!

And where did that awful name come from? Despite the numerous and amusing apocryphal stories, the truth is that the co-founders of NLP – Grinder and Bandler – were in a log cabin high in the hills behind Santa Cruz, pulling together the insights and discoveries that were to result in the book, *The Structure of Magic*. Towards the end of the marathon 36-hour session, they sat down with a bottle of Californian white wine and asked themselves, 'What on earth shall we call it?'

Grinder says the result was '*Neuro* because the results we were discovering seemed to operate at the level of neurology; *Linguistic* because of the ways in which language patterns reveal and impact our neurology; and *Programming* because the new discoveries enable us to break free of the way we have been programmed by socialization, and offer us new choices.'

Appendix 5: Ground rules for effective meetings

Here are some ground rules we typically use in Synectics. Feel free to invent your own and use terms that are comfortable for you:

Use your pad to manage the meeting in your head.
Use in–out listening to record thoughts and avoid interrupting or forgetting.

Speak for easy listening.
Use headline and background, be succinct and you will often be heard.

Assume positive intent.
More often than not intention will be positive and you will get a better outcome.

Say what is behind questions.
Avoid forcing people to guess what is in your mind; come clean and be clear.

Suspend judgement.
Speculation and absurdity only work if you do truly suspend judgement.

▓ **Stay loose until rigour counts.**
Remember Einstein, 'Imagination is more important than knowledge', followed by 'If at first the idea is not absurd, then there is no hope for it'; evaluate carefully!

▓ **State concerns positively: 'How to...', 'I wish...', 'I need a way...'**
Giving direction leads the mind to seek answers; statements of why not tend to make it close down.

Appendix 6:
The IQ – Innovation Quotient

Creativity and innovation questionnaire

Circle the number matching your opinion in relation to the following questions:

1. How well do the leaders in different functional areas in your organization work together?

Not well at all   2 4 6 8 10   Very well

2. How effectively does your organization break down barriers between different functional areas so that ideas can be exchanged?

Not well at all   1 2 3 4 5   Very well

3. Does your organization have a formal approach for generating ideas and using creativity/innovation to address business issues?

Doesn't have it   1 3 5 7 9   Has it and uses it

4. How often do meetings at your company produce truly innovative results?

Never   2 4 6 8 10   Always

5. Does your company's mission statement specifically mention creativity and / or innovation?

No   0   5   Yes

6. How would you rate your organization's actual performance in making innovation happen?

Need to learn basics 1   2   3   4   5   Superior at innovation

7. How successful is your company in developing new products and getting them to market?

Not successful at all 1   2   3   4   5   Very successful

8. Does your organization have a budget for innovation?

There is no budget   There is a clearly
today   2   4   6   8   10   specified budget

9. Do you have formal programmes for innovation in your organization?

Not at all   1   2   3   4   5   Widely

10. To what extent do you have quantified goals for innovation and its impact on future performance?

Difficult to connect to   A number of goals
any quantified goals 1   2   3   4   5   link to it directly

11. How important do people see innovation to be in their day-to-day jobs?

Not important   1   2   3   4   5   Important

12. How well are champions of innovation supported in driving projects through to implementation?

Not well at all   1   2   3   4   5   Very well

13. Are senior people able to take risks?

Not at all   1   2   3   4   5   Yes

14. To what extent is innovation celebrated and rewarded?

Hardly at all   1   2   3   4   5   A great deal

15. To what degree do senior management encourage innovation by demonstrating that 'It's OK to fail'?

Hardly at all   1   2   3   4   5   A great deal

16. How well do senior executives demonstrate commitment to innovation in the face of high short-term pressure?

Not well at all   1   2   3   4   5   Very well

17. How well are champions of innovation supported overall within your organization?

Not well at all   2   4   6   8   10   Very well

18. To what extent are you open to learning from your competitors and other industries?

Not well at all   1   2   3   4   5   Very open

19. To what extent are your innovation projects managed by cross-functional teams?

Rarely   1   2   3   4   5   Almost always

20. How well does your organization recognize and exploit the diversity of people's talents?

Not well at all   1   2   3   4   5   Very well

Calculate your Innovation Quotient by adding your scores. Use this scale:

Less than 55 = Spectators
55–84 = Seekers
85 or more = Stars